R.S. I

Spai

¡ Para mi amiga Bethany !

CreateSpace, Charleston SC

For information, visit www.facebook.com/ricardoelyeti

Printed in the United States by CreateSpace, Charleston SC

ISBN 13: 978-1-9869-0641-8
ISBN 10: 1986906418

List of Abbreviations

adj.	adjective
adv.	adverb
conj.	conjunction
def. art.	definite article
f.	feminine noun
indef. art.	indefinite article
interj.	interjection
interr.	interrogative
m.	masculine noun
n.	noun (*m or f*)
poss.	possessive
pron.	pronoun
v.	verb
v. irr.	irregular verb

Spanish Cardinal Numbers

1	uno	27	veintisiete
2	dos	28	veintiocho
3	tres	29	veintinueve
4	cuatro	30	treinta
5	cinco	31	treinta y uno
6	seis	40	cuarenta
7	siete	50	cincuenta
8	ocho	60	sesenta
9	nueve	70	setenta
10	diez	80	ochenta
11	once	90	noventa
12	doce	100	cien
13	trece	101	ciento uno
14	catorce	200	doscientos
15	quince	300	trescientos
16	dieciséis	400	cuatrocientos
17	diecisiete	500	quinientos
18	dieciocho	600	seiscientos
19	diecinueve	700	setecientos
20	veinte	800	ochocientos
21	veintiuno	900	novecientos
22	veintidós	1,000	mil
23	veintitrés	1,001	mil uno
24	veinticuatro	2,000	dos mil
25	veinticinco	1,000,000	un millón
26	veintiséis		

English Cardinal Numbers

1	one	27	twenty-seven
2	two	28	twenty-eight
3	three	29	twenty-nine
4	four	30	thirty
5	five	31	thirty-one
6	six	40	fourty
7	seven	50	fifty
8	eight	60	sixty
9	nine	70	seventy
10	ten	80	eighty
11	eleven	90	ninety
12	twelve	100	one hunderd
13	thirteen	101	one hundred-one
14	fourteen	200	two hundred
15	fifteen	300	three hundred
16	sixteen	400	four hundred
17	seventeen	500	five hundred
18	eighteen	600	six hundred
19	nineteen	700	seven hundred
20	twenty	800	eight hundred
21	twenty-one	900	nine hundred
22	twenty-two	1,000	one thousand
23	twenty-three	1,001	one thousand one
24	twenty-four	2,000	two thousand
25	twenty-five	1,000,000	one million
26	twenty-six		

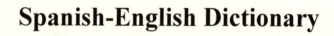

Spanish-English Dictionary

A

a *prep.* at; to
a veces *adv.* sometimes
abajo *prep., adv.* down
abecedario *m.* alphabet
abogado *n.* lawyer
abrazar *v.* hug
abrazo *m.* hug
abrigo *m.* coat
abril *m.* April
abuela *f.* grandmother
abuelo *m.* grandfather
abuelos *n.* grandparents
abundancia *f.* abundance
aburrido *adj.* bored; boring
acabar *v.* finish
acampar *v.* camp
accidente *m.* accident
aceptar *v.* accept
acerca de *prep.* about
aciete *m.* oil
acompañar *v.* accompany
acordar(se) *v. irr.* agree
acostar(se) *v. irr.* lie down
actitude *f.* attitude
actor *m.* actor
actriz *f.* actress
acuario *m.* aquarium
acuerdo *m.* agreement
adaptar(se) *v.* adapt
adelante *adv.* ahead; forward
adelante *adv.* forward
ademas *adv.* also
admirar *v.* admire
adoptar *v.* adopt
adulto *n.* adult

advertencia *f.* warning
advertir *v.* warn; caution
aeropuerto *m.* airport
afeitar(se) *v.* shave
agencia *f.* agency
agente *n.* agent
agosto *m.* August
agradecido *adj.* thankful
agricultura *f.* agriculture
agrio *adj.* sour
agua *m.* water
aguacate *m.* avocado
aguantar *v.* withstand
agudo *adj.* sharp
águila *m.* eagle
ahí *adv.* there
ahora *adv.* now
ahorrar *v.* save (money/things)
aire *m.* air
ajedrez *m.* chess
ajo *m.* garlic
ala *f.* wing
alambre *m.* wire
alarma *f.* alarm
alcanzar *v.* reach
alegre *adj.* happy
alergia *f.* allergy
alerta *adj.* alert
alfabeto *m.* alphabet
alfombra *f.* carpet; rug
alga marina *f.* seaweed
algo *m.* something
alguien *pron.* anybody; anyone

algún *adj., pron.* any
algún día *adv.* someday
alguno *pron.* anyone
algunos *pron., adj.* some
aliviar *v.* relieve
allá *adv.* there
allí *adv.* there
alma *f.* soul
almacén *m.* warehouse
almorzar *v. irr.* eat lunch
almuerzo *m.* lunch
alquien *pron.* somebody;
  someone
alquilar *v.* rent
alrededor *adv.* around
alto *adj.* tall; high
aluminio *m.* aluminum
amable *adj.* nice
amar *v.* love
amarillo *n., adj.* yellow
amarrar *v.* tie
ambición *f.* ambition
ambicioso *adj.* ambitious
ambos *adj., pron.* both
amenezar *v.* threaten
americano *adj.* American
amigo *n.* friend
amistoso *adj.* friendly
amor *m.* love
añadir *v.* add
anaranjado *adj.* orange
  (color)
ancho *adj.* wide
ángel *n.* angel
animal *m.* animal
animar *v.* cheer
año *m.* year
ansioso *adj.* anxious

antibiótico *m.* antibiotic
antiguo *adj.* antique;
  ancient
antipático *adj.* mean
apagar *v.* turn off
aparecer *v. irr.* appear
apio *m.* celery
aplastar *v.* crush; flatten
aplaudir *v.* clap
apreciar *v.* appreciate
aprender *v.* learn
aprobar *v. irr.*
  approve
apuntar *v.* take notes
aquél *adj.* that
aquella *adj.* that
aquí *adv.* here
araña *f.* spider
árbitro *n.* umpire
árbol *m.* tree
arco iris *m.* rainbow
argumento *m.* argument
armario *m.* closet
arquitecto *n.* architect
arrancar *v.* rip
arreglar *v.* fix; arrange
arrepentir *v.* regret
arriba *adv.* up; upstairs
arriba de *prep.* above
arriesgar *v.* jeopardize; risk
arroyo *n.* stream
arroz *m.* rice
arte *m.* art
artista *n.* artist
asiento *m.* seat
asistir a *v.* attend
asombrar(se) *v.* wonder
aspiración *f.* ambition

aspirina *f.* aspirin
asustado *adj.* scared
alacrán *m.* scorpion
asustar *v.* scare
atención *f.* attention
atleta *n.* athlete
atletismo *m.* track & field
atrapar *v.* catch; trap
aumentar *v.* increase
aunque *conj.* although; though
ausente *adj.* absent
autobús *m.* bus
autopista *f.* freeway
autor *n.* author
avenida *f.* avenue
aventura *f.* adventure
aventurero *adj.* adventurous
averiguar *v.* find out; check
avión *m.* airplane
avisar *v.* inform; advise; warn
aviso *m.* notice; advice; warning
avispa *f.* wasp
ayer *m., adj.* yesterday
ayuda *f.* help
ayudar *v.* help
azúcar *m.* sugar

B

bahía *f.* bay
bailar *v.* dance
bajar *v.* descend
ballet *m.* ballet
baloncesto *m.* basketball
bañar(se) *v.* bathe

banco *m.* bank
bandera *f.* flag
bañera *f.* bathtub
baño *m.* bathroom
barato *adj.* cheap
barba *f.* beard
barbilla *f.* chin
barco *m.* ship; boat
barranda *f.* railing
barrer *v.* sweep
barro *m.* clay
básico *adj.* basic
bastante *adj.* enough
bastón *m.* cane
basura *f.* trash
batería *f.* drum
batido *m.* shake
bebé *n.* baby
beber *v.* drink
bebida *f.* beverage; drink
beca *f.* scholarship
béisbol *m.* baseball
belleza *f.* beauty
biblioteca *f.* library
bicho *m.* bug
bicicleta *f.* bicycle
bien *adj.* good
bienvenido *adj.* welcome
bigote *m.* mustache
biología *f.* biology
bistec *m.* steak
blue jeans *m.* blue jeans
blusa *f.* blouse
boca *f.* mouth
bocadillo *m.* sandwich
boda *f.* wedding
boleto *m.* ticket
bolígrafo *m.* pen

bolsa *f.* bag; purse; pocket
bolsillo *m.* pocket
bonito *adj.* pretty; beautiful
borrar *v.* erase
borrego *m.* lamb
bosque *m.* forest
bota *f.* boot
botánica *f.* botany
bote *m.* boat
botella *f.* bottle
botón *m.* button
brazo *m.* arm
breve *adj.* short
brillante *adj.* bright
brillar *v.* shine
bronce *m.* bronze
bucear *v.* scuba dive
bueno *adj.* good
bufanda *f.* scarf
burro *m.* donkey
buscador *m.* search engine
buscar *v.* look for
ballena *f.* whale
barbas *f.* whiskers
blanco *n., adj.* white
bruja *f.* witch
bostezar *v.* yawn
bosteza *f.* yawn

C

caballero *m.* gentleman;
  cowboy
caballo *m.* horse
cabaña *f.* cabin
cabello *m.* hair
cabeza *f.* head
cable *m.* cable
cabra *f.* goat

cacahuate *m.* peanut
cacao *m.* cocoa
cacto *m.* cactus
cada *adj.* each
cadera *f.* hip
caer(se) *v. irr.* fall
café *n., adj.* brown;
  n. coffee
cajero *n.* cashier
calabacín *m.* zucchini
calabaza *f.* pumpkin
calaca *f.* skeleton
calavera *f.* skull
calcetín *m.* sock
calculadora *f.* calculator
calcular *v.* calculate
calendario *m.* calendar
calentar(se) *v. irr.* warm
calidad *f.* quality
caliente *adj.* hot
calificación *f.* qualification
callado *adj.* quiet
calle *m.* street
calor *m.* hot (weather)
caluroso *adj.* warm
calvo *adj.* bald
calzones *m.* underwear
cama *f.* bed
cámara *f.* camera
camarero *n.* waiter
camarón *m.* shrimp
cambiar *v.* change; switch
caminar *v.* walk
caminata *f.* hike; long
  walk; stroll
camino *m.* road
camión *m.* truck; bus
camisa *f.* shirt

camiseta *f.* t-shirt
campana *f.* bell
campión *n.* champion
campionato *m.*
  championship
canal *m.* canal; channel
canasta *f.* basket
cancelar *v.* cancel
cáncer *m.* cancer
canción *f.* song
canela *f.* cinnamon
cangrejo *m.* crab
canoa *f.* canoe
canoso *adj.* grey haired
cansado *adj.* tired
cansar(se) *v.* tire
cantante *n.* singer
cantar *v.* sing
cantidad *f.* quantity
cañón *m.* canyon
capital *f.* capital
capitán *n.* captain
capítulo *m.* chapter
cara *f.* face
caracol *m.* snail
caramelo *m.* caramel
cárcel *m.* jail
cargar *v.* carry
caricatura *f.* cartoon
caridad *f.* charity
cariñoso *adj.* affectionate;
  warmhearted; kind
carnaval *m.* carnival
carne *m.* meat
carnicería *f.* butcher shop
carpeta *f.* folder
carpintero *m.* carpenter
carrera *f.* career; race

carretera *f.* freeway
carro *m.* car
carrusel *m.* carousel
carta *f.* letter
cartel *m.* poster
cartelera *f.* billboard
cartera *f.* wallet
cartón *m.* cardboard
casa *f.* house; home
casar(se) *v.* marry
cascada *f.* waterfall
casi *adv.* almost
castillo *m.* castle
catedral *f.* cathedral
causa *f.* cause
caverna *f.* cavern
cazar *v.* hunt
cebolla *f.* onion
cebra *f.* zebra
ceja *f.* eyebrow
celebración *f.* celebration
celebrar *v.* celebrate
celoso *adj.* jealous
cementerio *m.* cemetary
cena *f.* dinner
cenar *v.* eat dinner
centavo *m.* cent
centígrado *m.* centigrade
centimetro *m.* centimeter
central *adj.* central
centro comercial *m.*
  shopping center; mall
centro *m.* downtown; center
cepillo *m.* brush
cera *f.* wax
cerámica *f.* ceramic
cerca *adj.* close
cerca *prep.* near

cercano *adj.* close
cerdo *m.* pig
cereal *m.* cereal
cerebro *m.* brain
ceremonia *f.* ceremony
cereza *f.* cherry
cero *n.* zero
cerrado *adj.* closed
cerrar(se) *v. irr.* close
cerro *m.* hill
certeza *f.* certainty
certificado *m.* certificate
césped *m.* lawn; grass
chal *m.* shawl
champú *m.* shampoo
chaqueta *m.* jacket
charco *m.* puddle
charka *f.* pond
charlar *v.* chat
cheque *m.* check
chica *f.* girl
chico *m.* boy
chile *m.* chile
chimenea *f.* chimney
chiquito *adj.* small
chisme *m.* gossip
chismoso *adj.* gossiper
chistoso *adj.* funny
chocar *v.* crash; hate
chocolate *m.* chocolate
chofer *n.* driver
chorizo *m.* sausage
cicatriz *m.* scar
ciclismo *f.* cycling
cielo *f.* heaven; sky
ciencias *f.* science
ciencias sociales *f.* social science

científico *n.* scientist
ciertamente *adv.* certainly
cierto *adj.* sure; certain; true
cine *m.* movie theater
cinta *f.* tape
cintura *f.* waist
cinturón *m.* belt
círculo *m.* circle
ciruela *f.* plum
cirugía *f.* surgury
cirujano *n.* surgeon
ciudad *f.* city
ciudadanía *f.* citizenship
ciudadano *n.* citizen
claro *adj.* clear; bright
clase *f.* class
cliente *n.* client; customer
clima *f.* climate; weather
clínica *f.* clinic
cobija *f.* blanket
cobre *m.* copper
coche *m.* car
cochino *m.* pig
cocina *f.* kitchen
cocinar *v.* cook
cocinero *n.* cook
coco *m.* coconut
cocodrilo *m.* crocodile
codo *m.* elbow
coger *v.* grab; take
cohete *m.* rocket
cola *f.* tail
colección *n.* collection
coleccionar *v.* collect
colegio *m.* school; high school; college
colgar *v. irr.* hang

color *m.* color
colorear *v.* color
combinación *f.*
   combination
combinar *v.* combine
comedia *f.* comedy
comedor *m.* dining room
comenzar *v. irr.* begin; start
comercial *m.* commercial
comestible *adj.* edible
comestibles *m.* groceries
cómico *adj.* funny
comida *f.* food
comienzo *m.* beginning
cómo *adv.* how; *inter.* how?
como *conj., adv.* as
compacto *adj.* compact
compañero *n.* companion
compañía *f.* company
comparar *v.* compare
compartimiento *m.*
   compartment
compartir *v.* share
compás *m.* compass
competencia *f.* competition
competir *v.* compete
complemento *m.*
   complement
completo *adj.* complete
complicar *v.* complicate
comportamiento *m.*
   behavior
comprar *v.* buy; purchase
comprender *v.* understand;
   comprehend
computación *f.* computer
   science
computadora *f.* computer

común *adj.* common
comunicar *v.* communicate
comunidad *f.* community
con *prep.* with
concha *f.* shell
concierto *m.* concert
condición *f.* condition
conducir *v. irr.* drive
conectar *v.* connect
conejo *m.* rabbit
confesar *v.* confess
confianza *f.* confidence;
   trust
confirmar *v.* confirm
confundir *v.* confuse
conseguir *v. irr.* get
consejo *m.* advice
conservar *v.* conserve
considerado *adj.*
   considerate; thoughtful
considerar *v.* consider
construir *v.* construct
contaminación *f.*
   contamination
contar *v.* count
contento *adj.* happy;
   content
continuar *v.* continue
contra *prep.* against
contribuir *v.* contribute
controlar *v.* control
conversación *f.*
   conversation
copiar *v.* copy
corazón *m.* heart
calentar *v. irr.* heat
corbata *f.* tie
cordero *m.* lamb

coro *m.* choir
corredor *m.* hallway
corregir *v. irr.* correct
correo electrónico *m.* email
correo *m.* mail; post office
correr *v.* run
cortado *adj.* cut
cortadura *f.* cut
cortar *v.* cut
cortina *f.* curtain
corto *adj.* short (length)
cosa *f.* thing
cosechar *v.* harvest
coser *v.* sow
cosquillear *v.* tickle
costa *f.* coast
costar *v.* cost
costilla *f.* rib
costo *m.* cost
costra *f.* scab
costumbre *m.* custom; habit
crayón *m.* crayon
crear *v.* create
creativo *adj.* creative
crecer *v. irr.* grow
creer *v.* believe
creíble *adj.* believable;
  credible
crema de cacahuate (maní)
  f. peanut butter
crema *f.* cream
criar *v.* raise
criatura *f.* creature
crimen *m.* crime
cristal *m.* crystal
crucigrama *f.* crossword
  puzzle
crudo *adj.* uncooked

cruz *f.* cross
cruzar *v.* cross
cuaderno *m.* notebook
cuadra *f.* city block, frame
cuadrado *adj., n.* square
cuál *pron.* which
cualquiera *adj.* either
cualquiera *pron.* whichever
cuando *adv., conj.* when
cuándo *interr.* when?
cuánto *inter.* How much?
cuántos *inter.* How many?
cuarto *m.* room; *m.,*
  adj. one quarter; fourth
cuchara *f.* spoon
cuchichear *v.* whisper
cuchicheo *m.* whisper
cuchillo *m.* knife
cuello *m.* neck
collar *m.* necklace
cuenta *f.* bill; account; score
cuento *m.* story
cuerda *f.* rope
cuerpo *m.* body
cuervo *m.* raven
cueva *f.* cave
cuidadoso *adj.* careful
culebra *f.* snake
culpa *f.* fault
cultura *f.* culture
cumbre *m.* summit
cumpleaños *m.* birthday
cuñada *f.* sister-in-law
cura *f.* cure
curiosidad *f.* curiosity
curioso *adj.* curious
curita *f.* bandaid
curva *f.* curve

D

dama *f.* lady
dañar *v.* harm
dar *v. irr.* give
de *prep.* from
debajo *adv.* underneath
debajo de *prep.* below;
  beneath
deber *v.* should; must
débil *adj.* weak
debilidad *f.* weakness
decedir *v.* decide
decir *v. irr.* say
decoración *f.* decoration
decorar *v.* decorate
dejar *v.* quit
deletrear *v.* spell
delfín *m.* dolphin
delgado *adj.* skinny; thin
delicado *adj.* delicate;
  sensitive
delicioso *adj.* delicious
demasiado *adv.* too much;
  excessive
democracia *f.* decmocracy
demonstrar *v. irr.*
  demonstrate
denso *adj.* dense
dentista *n.* dentist
deportar *v.* deport
deporte *m.* sport
depresión *f.* depression
derecho *adj.* straight
derechos *adj.* rights
desaparecer *v. irr.* disappear
desayunar *v.* eat breakfast
desayuno *m.* breakfast

descansar *v.* rest
descargar *v.* download
descontinuar *v.* discontinue
descortés *adj.* impolite
describir *v.* describe
descubrir *v.* discover
descuento *m.* discount
desde *prep.* from
desear *v.* wish
deseo *m.* wish
desfile *m.* parade
desierto *m.* desert
desihidratar *v.* dehydrate
desnutrición *f.* malnutrition
desobedecer *v.* disobey
desocupado *adj.* vacant;
  empty
despacio *adj.* slow
desperdiciar *v.* waste
despertar(se) *v. irr.* awake
después *prep.* after
detrás de *prep.* behind
día *m.* day
diálogo *m.* dialogue
diamante *m.* diamond
diario *m.* journal; diary;
  adj. daily; everyday
dibujar *v.* draw
diccionario *m.* dictionary
dicho *m.* saying
diciembre *m.* December
diente *m.* tooth
diferencia *f.* difference
diferente *adj.* different
difícil *adj.* difficult; tough
digestión *f.* digestion
dinero *m.* money

dirección *f.* direction, address

directo *adj.* direct

disco *m.* disk

disculpar(se) *v.* apologize

discusión *f.* discussion

disfrutar *v.* enjoy

disinfectante *m.* disinfectant

distancia *f.* distance

distinto *adj.* distinct; different

distraer *v. irr.* distract

divertido *v.* fun

dividir(se) *v.* divide; split

doblar *v.* fold

docena *f.* dozen

doctor *n.* doctor

documento *m.* document

dólar *m.* dollar

doler(se) *v. irr.* hurt, ache

dolor *m.* pain, ache

domingo *n.* Sunday

donde *adv.* where

dónde *interr.* where?

dondequiera *adv.* wherever

dormido *adj.* asleep

dormir(se) *v. irr.* fall asleep

dormitorio *m.* bedroom

drama *f.* drama

droga *f.* drug

ducha *f.* shower

duchar(se) *v.* shower

duda *f.* doubt

dudar *v.* doubt

dulce *adj.* sweet *m.* candy

dulcería *f.* candy store

durante *prep.* during

duro *adj.* hard; tough

DVD *m.* DVD

E

eco *m.* echo

ecológico *adj.* ecological

economia *f.* economy

económico *adj.* economic

edad *f.* age

edeficio *m.* building

editar *v.* edit

educación *f.* education

educar *v.* educate; teach

efectivo *adj.* effective; *n.* cash

efectuar *v.* effect

eficiente *adj.* efficient

egoísta *adj.* selfish

ejemplo *m.* example

ejercicio *m.* exercise

el *def. art.* the; *pron.* who

él mismo *pron.* himself

él *pron.* he

electricidad *f.* electricity

elefante *m.* elephant

elegante *adj.* elegant

elegir *v. irr.* elect

ella *pron.* she

ellos *def. art.* they; them

elote *m.* corn (on the cob)

emigrar *v.* emigrate

emoción *f.* emotion

emocionado *adj.* excited; emotional

empacar *v.* pack

emparedado *m.* sandwich

empezar *v. irr.* start

empleado *n.* employee
emplear *v.* employ
en línea *prep.* online
en medio *prep.* among; in
  the middle
en *prep.* in; on; at; into; onto
encarcelar *v.* jail
encender *v. irr.* power on
encendido *adj.* power on
encima *prep.* over; on top
encontrar(se) *v. irr.* meet;
  find
endurecer(se) *v. irr.* toughen
energía *f.* energy
enero *m.* January
enfermedad *f.* sickness;
  illness
enfermo *adj.* sick; *m.* sick
engañar *v.* cheat
engeniero *n.* engineer
enojado *adj.* mad
enorme *adj.* enormous;
  huge
ensalada *f.* salad
enseñar *v.* teach; show
entender *v. irr.* understand
entero *adj.* entire; whole;
  intact
entonces *adv.* then
entrada *f.* entrance
entre *prep.* between
entregar *v.* deliver; turn in
entusiasmo *m.* enthusiasm
enviar *v.* send
episodio *m.* episode
equipaje *m.* luggage
equipo *m.* equipment; team
equivocar(se) *v.* mistake

error *m.* error
erupción *n.* eruption
eruptir *v.* erupt
escalera *f.* stairs; ladder
escándalo *m.* scandal
escoba *f.* broom
escojer *v.* choose
esconder(se) *v.* hide
escritorio *m.* desk
escuchar *v.* listen
escuela *f.* school
esculpir *v.* sculpt
escultor *n.* sculptor
escultura *f.* sculpture
ese *adj.* that
esfuerzo *m.* effort
espacio *m.* space
espada *f.* sword
espagueti *m.* spaghetti
espalda *f.* back; spine
español *m.* Spanish
espantar *v.* scare
esparanza *f.* hope
especia *f.* spice
especial *adj.* special
especialidad *f.* specialty
especialista *n.* specialist
especializar(se) *v.*
  specialize
especialmente *adv.*
  especially
especie *m.* species
especificar *v.* specify
espectacular *adj.*
  spectacular
espejo *m.* mirror
esperar *v.* wait
espiar *v.* spy

espinaca *f.* spinach
espinilla *f.* shin
espíritu *m.* spirit
esponja *f.* sponge
esposa *f.* wife
esposo *m.* husband; spouse
esqueleto *m.* skeleton
esquí *m.* skiing
esquiar *v.* ski
esquina *f.* corner
estación *f.* season; station
estacionamiento *m.* parking
estacionar *v.* park
estadio *m.* stadium
estado *m.* state
estampilla *f.* stamp
estanque *m.* pond; tank
estante *m.* shelf
estantería *f.* bookshelf
estar *v. irr.* be
estatua *f.* statue
este *adj.* this; *m.* east
estilo *m.* style
estimar *v.* estimate
estirar(se) *v.* stretch
estornudar *v.* sneeze
estornudo *m.* sneeze
estos *adj.* these
éstos *pron.* these
estrategia *f.* strategy
estrella *f.* star
estricto *adj.* strict
estudiante *n.* student
estudiar *v.* study
estudio *m.* study
estufa *f.* stove
ético *adj.* ethical
evacuación *f.* evacuation

evaluar *v.* evaluate
evidencia *f.* evidence
evitar *v.* avoid
exacto *adj.* exact
exageración *f.* exaggeration
examen *m.* test
examinar *v.* examine; test
excelente *adj.* excellent
existir *v.* exist
éxito *m.* success
expedición *f.* expedition
experiencia *f.* experience
experimento *m.* experiment
explicación *f.* explanation
explicar *v.* explain
exploración *f.* exploration
explorador *n.* explorer
explorar *v.* explore
explosion *f.* explosion
extincto *adj.* extinct
extra *adj.* extra
extranjero *adj.* foreign;
  n. foreigner
extraño *adj.* strange
extremo *adj.* extreme

F

fabuloso *v.* fabulous
fácil *adj.* easy
falda *f.* skirt
fallar *v.* fail
falso *adj.* false
fama *f.* fame
familia *f.* family
familiar *adj.* familiar
famoso *adj.* famous
fantasma *f.* ghost
farmacia *f.* pharmacy

fascinar (le) *adj.* fascinated
fastidiar *v.* annoy
favor *m.* favor
favorito *adj.* favorite
fé *f.* faith
febrero *m.* February
fecha *f.* date
federal *m.* federal
felicitación *f.* congratulation
feliz *adj.* happy
femenino *adj.* feminine
fenomenal *adj.*
   phenomenal; great
feo *adj.* ugly
ferrocarril *m.* railroad;
   railway
ficción *f.* fiction
fiebre *m.* fever
fiesta *f.* party; festival
fin *m.* end
final *adj., m.* final; last
finalmente *adv.* finally; last
flaco *adj.* skinny
flauta *f.* flute
flexible *adj.* flexible
flojo *adj.* lazy
flor *f.* flower
foca *f.* seal
folleto *m.* pamphlet
forma *f.* shape
formar *v.* shape
forzar *v.* forcé
fotografía *f.* photograph
frágil *adj.* fragile
frambuesa *f.* rasberry
francés *m.* French
frase *f.* frase
frecuente *adj.* frequent

fregadero *m.* sink
frente *m.* front
fresa *f.* strawberry
fresco *adj.* cool; fresh
frijoles *m.* beans
frío *m., adj.* cold
fruita *f.* fruit
frustrado *adj.* frustrated
fuego *m.* fire
fuente *f.* fountain
fuera *prep., adv.* out
fuerte *adj.* strong; loud
fuerza *f.* strength; force
fumar *v.* smoke
funcionar *v.* function
fútbol americano *m.*
   football
fútbol *m.* soccer

G

gafas *f.* glasses
galaxia *f.* Galaxy
galleta *f.* cookie; cracker
gallo *m.* rooster
galón *m.* gallon
ganador *n.* winner
ganar *v.* win, earn
ganso *m.* goose
garaje *m.* garaje
garganta *m.* throat
gasolina *f.* gas
gastado *adj.* worn
gaviota *f.* seagull
generoso *adj.* generous
geografía *f.* geography
gigante *adj.* giant
gimnasia *f.* gimnastics
gimnasio *m.* gym

gobernador *n.* governor
golf *m.* golf
golpe *m.* hit
golpear *v.* hit
gomma de borrar *f.* eraser
gordo *adj.* fat
gorro/a *n.* hat
grado *m.* degree (temp);
  grade level (school)
grande *adj.* big
granero *m.* barn
granizo *m.* hail
granja *f.* farm
grillo *m.* cricket
gris *adj.* grey
gritar *v.* scream, shout, yell
grito *m.* scream, shout, yell
gruta *f.* grave
guacamole *m.* guacamole
guante *m.* glove
guapo *adj.* handsome
guardar *v.* keep; save
guerrero *n.* warrior
guitara *f.* guitar
gusano *m.* worm
gustar *v.* like

H

habitación *f.* room; habitat
hábitat *m.* habitat
hablar *v.* talk; speak
hacer *v. irr.* make; do
hacer(se) *v. irr.* become
hacia *prep.* to
hacienda *f.* estate; ranch
hambre *m.* hunger
hamburguesa *f.* hamburger
harina *f.* flour

hasta *prep.* to; till; until
helado *m.* ice cream
helicóptero *m.* helicopter
hembra *f.* female
hermano *m.* brother
hermoso *adj.* beautiful
héroe *n.* hero
heroico *adj.* heroic
herramienta *f.* tool
hielo *m.* ice
hija *f.* daughter
hijo *m.* son
histérico *adj.* hysterical
historia *f.* history; story
hogar *m.* home
hola *int.* hello
hombre *m.* man
hombro *m.* shoulder
hondo *adj.* deep
honesto *adj.* honest
honrado *adj.* honest;
  honorable
hora *f.* hour; time
horario *m.* schedule
hormiga *f.* ant
horror *m.* horror
hospital *m.* hospital
hotel *m.* hotel
hoy *n., adv.* today
hueso *m.* bone
huevo *m.* egg
húmedo *adj.* humid

I

idea *f.* idea
idéntico *adj.* identical
identificación *f.*
  identification

iglesia *f.* church
igual *adj.* same
igual *m.* equal; same
igualar *v.* equal
ilusión *f.* illusion
imaginar *v.* imagine
imaginativo *adj.*
  imaginative
imitar *v.* imitate
impaciente *adj.* impatient
impermeable *m.* raincoat
importancia *f.* importance
importante *adj.* important
imposible *adj.* imposible
impresora *f.* printer
imprimir *v.* print
inaceptable *adj.*
  unacceptable
incapaz *adj.* unable
incómodo *adj.*
  uncomfortable
incompleto *adj.* incomplete
incorrecto *adj.* incorrect
increíble *adj.* incredible
independencia *f.*
  independence
indígena *f.* indigenous
indigestión *f.* indigestion
individuo *m.* individual
inevitable *adj.* unavoidable
infección *f.* infection
infectar *v.* infect
inflar *v.* inlfate
información *f.* information
informar *v.* inform
infrecuente *adj.* infrequent
inmaduro *adj.* immature
inmenso *adj.* immense

inmigrar *v.* immigrate
inocente *adj.* innocent
inquieto *adj.* anxious
insecto *m.* insect
inservible *adj.* useless
inspección *f.* inspection
inspiración *f.* inspiration
instrucción *f.* instruction
insulina *f.* insulin
inteligente *adj.* inteligent
interés *m.* interest
interesante *adj.* interesting
internet *m.* internet
introducir *v. irr.* introduce
inútil *adj.* useless
investigar *v.* investigate
invierno *m.* winter
invisible *adj.* invisible
invitación *f.* invitation
invitar *v.* invite
ir *v. irr.* go
irse *v.* to leave
isla *f.* island
itinerario *m.* itinerary

J

jabón *m.* soap
jaguar *m.* jaguar
jalar *v.* pull
jalea *f.* jelly
jamás *adv.* never
jamón *m.* ham
jardín *adj.* garden; yard
jarra *f.* jar
jazz *m.* jazz
jitomate *m.* tomato
joyas *f.* jewelry
joyería *f.* jewelry store

juego *m.* game
juez *n.* judge
jugador *n.* player
jugar *v. irr.* play
jugo *m.* juice
julio *m.* July
junio *m.* June
juntar(se) *v.* assemble; gather
junto *adv.* together
justificar *v.* justify
justo *adj.* fair
juzgar *v.* judge

K

kilogramo *m.* kilogram
kilómetro *m.* kilometer

L

labio *m.* lip
ladrar *v.* bark
ladrón *n.* burglar
lágrima *f.* tear
laguna *f.* lagoon
lana *f.* wool
langosta *f.* lobster
lápiz *m.* pencil
largo *adj.* long
lavamanos *m.* sink
lavar(se) *v.* wash
lección *f.* lesson
leche *f.* milk
lechuga *f.* lettuce
lechuza *f.* owl
lectura *f.* reading
leer *v.* read
legal *adj.* legal
legítimo *adj.* legitimate; true
legumbre *m.* vegetable

lejos *adj.* far
lengua *f.* tongue
lenguaje *m.* language
lentes *m.* glasses
lento *adj.* slow
león *m.* lion
letra *f.* letter
levantar(se) *v.* lift; get up
leyenda *f.* legend
libertad *f.* liberty
libertar *v.* set free
libra *f.* pound
libre *adj.* free
librería *f.* bookstore
líder *n.* leader
lima *f.* lime
limitar *v.* limit
limón *m.* lemon
limonada *f.* lemonade
limpiar *v.* clean
lindo *adj.* pretty; lovely; cute
línea *f.* line
liquido *m.* liquid
lista *f.* list
listo *adj.* ready; smart
literatura *f.* literature
llama *f.* flame
llamar *v.* call
llave *m.* key
llegar *v.* arrive
llenar *v.* to fill
lleno *adj.* full
llevar *v.* wear; carry; take
llorar *v.* cry
llover *v. irr.* rain
lluvia *f.* rain
lluvioso *adj.* rainy

lobo *m.* wolf
loción *f.* lotion
loco *adj.* crazy
lograr *v.* achieve
lombriz *m.* worm
loro *m.* parrot
luchar *v.* fight; wrestle; struggle
luego *adj.* next
luego *adv.* then
lugar *m.* place
luna *f.* moon
luz *f.* light

M

madera *f.* wood
madre *f.* mother
madrina *f.* godmother
madurar *v.* mature
maduro *adj.* mature; ripe
maestro *n.* teacher
mágica *f.* magic
magnético *m.* magnetic
magnífico *adj.* grand
maíz *m.* corn
malo *adj.* bad
maltratar *v.* mistreat
mamá *f.* mom
mañana *f.* morning; tomorrow
mancha *f.* stain; spot
mandar *v.* send
mandíbula *f.* jaw
manejar *v.* drive
manera *f.* manner
mango *m.* mango
mano *f.* hand
mantener *v. irr.* maintain

mantequilla *f.* butter
manzana *f.* apple
mapa *m.* map
mapache *m.* racoon
máquina *f.* machine
mar *n.* sea
maravillar(se) *v.* wonder
maravilloso *adj.* marvelous; amazing
marca *f.* mark
marcador *m.* marker
marcar *v.* mark; dial (phone)
marchar *v.* march
mareo *m.* seasickness
marina *f.* marina
marinero *n.* sailor
mariposa *f.* butterfly
marisco *m.* shellfish
martes *m.* Tuesday
marzo *m.* March
más *n., adv., adj.* more
mascota *f.* pet
masculino *adj.* masculine
masticar *v.* chew
matemáticas *f.* math
material *m.* material
matrimonio *m.* marriage
mayo *m.* May
mayoría *f.* majority
me *pron.* me
mecánico *n.* mechanic
medalla *f.* medal
medicina *f.* medecine
médico *n.* doctor
medida *f.* measurement
medio ambiente *m.* environment

medio *m., adj.* middle
mediodía *f.* noon
medir *v. irr.* measure
mejilla *f.* cheek
mejor *adj.* best; better
mejorar *v.* improve
melodía *f.* melody
memoria *f.* memory
mencionar *v.* mention
menor *adj.* younger
menor *m.* minor
menos *adj.* less; least; *adv.* minus; *prep.* except for
mensaje *m.* message
mentir *v. irr.* lie
menú *m.* menu
mercado *m.* market
merecer *v. irr.* deserve; earn
merendar(se) *v.irr.* snack
mes *m.* month
mesa *f.* table
metal *m.* metal
metro *m.* subway
mezcla *f.* mix
mezclar(se) *v.* mix
mi *adj.* my
microonda *f.* microwave
miedo *m.* fear
miedoso *adj.* afraid
miel *f.* honey
miembro *n.* member
mientras *conj.* while; meanwhile
miércoles *m.* Wednesday
migrar *v.* migrate
milagro *m.* miracle
mirada *f.* look
mirar *v.* look; watch

misión *f.* mission
mismo *adj.* same
misterio *m.* mystery
mochila *f.* backpack
modelar *v.* model
modelo *m.* model
moderno *adj.* modern
modo *m.* style
mojar(se) *v.* wet
molestar *v.* bother
momento *m.* moment
moneda *f.* coin
mono *adj.* cute; pretty *m.* monkey
monopatín *m.* skateboard
monstruo *m.* monster
montaña *f.* mountain
monte *m.* mountain
morado *n., adj.* purple
moreno *adj.* dark hair
morir *v. irr.* die
morsa *f.* walrus
mosca *f.* fly
mosquito *m.* mosquito
mostrar(se) *v. irr.* show; demonstrate
motocicleta *f.* motorcycle
mover *v. irr.* move
muchacha *f.* girl
muchacho *m.* boy
mucho *adv.* very
mucho *n., adv., adj.* very; much; a lot
muchos *adj.* many
mudar *v.* move
muerte *f.* death
muerto *adj.* dead
mujer *f.* woman

multiplicación *f.* multiplication
mundo *m.* world
muñeca *f.* wrist
muñeco *m.* doll
murciélago *m.* bat
músculo *m.* muscle
museo *m.* museum
música *f.* music
músico *n.* musician
muslo *m.* thigh
muy *adv.* very, much

N

nación *f.* nation
nada *pron.* none; nothing
nadar *v.* swim
nadie *n., adj.* nobody
naranja *f.* orange (fruit)
nariz *f.* nose
natación *f.* swimming
naturaleza *adj.* nature
náusea *f.* nausea
náutico *adj.* nautical
navegador *m.* browser
navegar *v.* navegate
navidad *f.* christmas
neblina *f.* fog
necesario *adj.* necessary
necesitar *v.* need
negativo *adj., n.* negative
negocio *m.* business
nervioso *adj.* nervous
nevar *v. irr.* snow
ni *conj.* nor
niebla *f.* fog
nieto *n.* grandchild
nieve *f.* snow

ninguno *pron.* neither
niña *f.* girl
niño *m.* boy; child
no *n., adj.* no; *adv.* not
noche *f.* night
nombre *m.* name
normal *adj.* normal
normalmente *adv.* normally
norte *m.* north
nosotros *pron.* we; us
nota *f.* note; grade (school report)
notar *v.* note
noticias *f.* news
notificar *v.* notify
novena *f., adj.* ninth
novia *f.* girlfriend
noviembre *m.* November
novio *m.* boyfriend
nube *m.* cloud
nublado *adj.* cloudy
nuestro *adj.* our
nuevo *adj.* new
nuez *m.* nut
número *m.* number
numerosos *adj.* numerous
nunca *adv.* never
nutrición *f.* nutrition

O

obligatorio *adj.* mandatory
obscuro *adj.* dark
obtener *v. irr.* get; obtain
ocupado *adj.* busy
ocurrir *v.* occur
oeste *m.* west
oír *v. irr.* listen; hear
ojo *m.* eye

ola *f.* wave
oler *v. irr.* smell
olvidar(se) *v.* forget
oportunidad *f.* oportunity
oración *f.* sentence
oreja *f.* ear
orgullo *m.* pride
orgulloso *adj.* proud
orilla *f.* edge
oro *m.* gold
ortografía *f.* spelling
oruga *f.* caterpillar
oso *m.* bear
otoño *m.* fall
otra *adj.* another
otra vez *adv.* again
oveja *f.* sheep

P

¿por qué? *inter.* why?
padre *m.* father
padres *m.* parents
padrino *m.* godfather
padrinos *m.* godparents
pagar *v.* pay
página *f.* page
país *m.* country
paisaje *m.* scenery; landscape
paja *f.* hay
paja *f.* hat; straw (grass)
pájaro *m.* bird
palabra *f.* word
pálido *adj.* pale
palma *f.* palm tree
palmera *f.* palm tree
palo *m.* stick
pan *m.* bread

panadería *f.* bakery
pánico *m.* panic
pantalla *f.* screen (device)
pantalones cortos *m.* shorts
pantalones *m.* pants
pañuelo *m.* tissue
papa *f.* potato
papá *m.* dad
papas fritas *f.* french fries
papaya *f.* papaya
papel *m.* paper
papitas *f.* potato chips
paquete *m.* package
par *m.* pair
para *prep.* for
paraguas *m.* umbrela
paraíso *m.* paradise
parar *v.* stop
parecido *adj.* similar
pared *f.* wall
pareja *f.* couple; pair
pariente *m.* relative
parque *m.* park
párrafo *m.* paragraph
participar *v.* participate
partido *m.* game
pasa *f.* raisin
pasajero *n.* passenger
pasar *v.* happen; pass; spend (time)
pasillo *m.* hallway
pastel *m.* cake
patata *f.* potato
patinar *v.* skate
patio *m.* patio
pato *m.* duck
pavo *m.* turkey
payaso *n.* clown

pedir *v. irr.* ask
pegajoso *adj.* sticky
pegamento *m.* glue
pegante *m.* glue
pegar *v.* glue; hit
peinar *v.* comb
peine *m.* comb
pelea *f.* fight
pelear *v.* fight
película *f.* movie; film
peligro *m.* danger
peligroso *adj.* dangerous
pelirrojo *adj.* red-headed
pelo *m.* hair
pelota *f.* ball
peluquero *n.* barber
pensar *v. irr.* think
pensativo *adj.* thoughtful
peor *adj.* worse
pequeño *adj.* little; small
pera *f.* pear
perder *v. irr.* lose
pérdida *f.* waste; loss
perdido *adj.* lost
perdonar *v.* forgive
perezoso *adj.* lazy
periodista *n.* journalist
permitir *v.* permit, allow
pero *conj.* but
perro *m.* dog
perseguir *v. irr.* follow
pesado *adj.* heavy
pesar *v.* weigh
pescadería *f.* fish market
pescado *m.* fish (cooked)
pescar *v.* fish
peso *n.* weight
pestaña *f.* eyelash

petróleo *m.* oil
pez *m.* fish (alive)
piano *m.* piano
picante *adj.* spicy
pie *m.* foot
piedra *f.* stone; rock
piel *f.* skin
pierna *f.* leg
pila *f.* battery
piloto *n.* pilot
pingüino *m.* penguin
pintar *v.* paint
pintura *f.* paint; painting
piña *f.* pineapple
pirámide *m.* pyramid
piscina *f.* pool
piso *m.* floor
placer *m.* pleasure
plan *m.* plan
planear *v.* plan
planeta *m.* planet
plano *adj.* flat
planta *f.* plant
plantar *v.* plant
plástico *m.* plastic
plata *f.* silver
plátano *m.* banana
platicar *v.* tall; chat
plato *m.* plate
playa *f.* beach
pluma *f.* pen ; feather
plural *m., adj.* plural
pobre *adj.* poor
pobreza *f.* poverty
poco *adj.* few
poema *m.* poem
poeta *n.* poet
policía *n.* police

pollo *m.* chicken
polución *f.* polution
pomada *f.* ointment
poner(se) *v. irr.* put
popote *m.* straw (drink)
popular *adj.* popular
por ciento *m.* percent
por fin *adv.* finally
por *prep.* from; for; via; through
por que *adv.* why
por último *adv.* finally
porcelana *n.* porcelain
porque *conj.* because
posible *adj.* possible
posición *f.* position
positivo *adj.* positive
póster *m.* poster
postre *m.* dessert
practicar *v.* practice
precaución *f.* precaution
precio *m.* price
preferencia *f.* preference
preferir *v. irr.* prefer
pregunta *f.* question
preguntar *v.* ask
premio *m.* award; prize
preocupado *adj.* worried; preocupied
preocupar(se) *v.* worry
preparer(se) *v.* prepare
preparatoria *f.* high School
prescribir *v.* prescribe
presentar *v.* present
presente *adj.* present
presidente *n.* president
prestar *v.* borrow
pretender *v.* pretend

primario *adj.* primary
primavera *f.* springtime
primer *m.* first
primero *adj.* first
primitivo *adj.* primitive
primo *n.* cousin
principal *adj.* principal
principio *m.* beginning
privado *adj.* private
probable *adj.* probable
probar(se) *v. irr.* test; taste; try; try on; prove
problema *m.* problem
procedimiento *m.* procedure
proceso *m.* process
producir *v. irr.* produce; create
producto *m.* product
profesión *f.* profession
profesor *n.* professor
profundidad *f.* depth
profundo *adj.* deep
programa *m.* software; program
progreso *m.* progress
prohibir *v.* prohibit
promesa *f.* promise
prometer *v.* promise
pronto *adv.* soon
pronunciar *v.* pronounce
propiedad *f.* property
propina *f.* tip (service)
propósito *m.* purpose
proteger *v.* protect
proveer *v.* provide
próximo *adj.* next
proyecto *m.* project

prueba *f.* proof; quiz
psiquiatra *n.* phsychiatrist
publicar *v.* publish
público *m., adj,* public
pueblo *m.* town
puente *m.* bridge
puerco *m.* pig; pork
puerta *f.* door
puerto *m.* harbor
pues *adv.* well
pulgada *f.* inch
pulgar *m.* thumb
pulmonar *n.* pulmonary
pulso *m.* pulse
punta *f.* tip
pupitre *m.* desk (student)
puro *adj.* pure

Q

¿qué? *inter.* what?
¿quién(es)? *inter.* who
quebrado *adj.* broken
quebrar *v.* break
quedar(se) *v.* stay
quehaceres *m.* chores
queja *f.* complaint
quejar(se) *v.* complain
querer *v.* want
quien *pron.* whom
quienes *pron.* whose
quienquiera (que) *pron.*
  whomever
quinto *m., adj.* fifth
quitar(se) *v.* remove

R

rábano *m.* radish
racismo *m.* racism
racista *n.* racist

radio *f.* radio
radiografía *f.* x-ray
radiografiar *v.* x-ray
raíz *m.* root
rama *f.* branch
rana *n.* frog
rápidamente *adv.* fast
rápido *adj.* fast
raro *adj.* rare; strange
rascacielos *m.* skyscraper
rascar *v.* scratch
rasguñar *v.* scratch
rata *f.* rat
ratón *m.* mouse
raya *f.* stripe
rayado *adj.* striped
rayar *v.* scratch
razón *f.* reason; cause
razonable *adj.* reasonable
razonar *v.* reason
reacción *f.* reaction
real *adj.* real
realidad *f.* reality
realizar *v.* realize
realmente *adv.* really
receta *f.* recipe; prescription
recetar *v.* prescribe
recibir *v.* recieve
recibo *m.* receipt
reciente *adj.* recently
recordar *v. irr.* remember;
  remind
recreo *m.* recess
rectángulo *m.* rectangle
recto *adj.* straight
recurso *m.* resource
redondo *adj.* round
reembolsar *v.* refund

reembolso *m.* refund
referencia *m.* reference
reflejar *v.* reflect
refresco *m.* soda
refrigerador *m.* refrigerator
refugiado *n.* refugee
regalo *m.* gift; present
regañar *v.* scold
regatear *v.* bargain
región *f.* region
regla *f.* ruler; rule
regresar *v.* return
regular *adj.* regular
reina *f.* queen
reír(se) *v.* laugh
relajar(se) *v.* relax
reloj *m.* clock; watch
renta *f.* rent
reparar *v.* repair
repasar *v.* review
repetir(se) *v.* repeat
representante *n.*
  representative
repuesta *f.* reply; response
reservación *f.* reservation
reservar *v.* reserve
resistir *v.* resist
resolver *v. irr.* resolve
respetar *v.* respect
respeto *m.* respect
responder *v.* answer;
  respond
responsable *adj.*
  responsible
restaurante *m.* restaurant
resultado *m.* result
reunión *f.* reunion; meeting
reunir(se) *v.* assemble; meet

revista *f.* magazine
rey *m.* king
rico *adj.* delicious; rich
  (money)
riesgo *m.* risk
rifa *f.* raffle
rígido *adj.* stiff
riñón *m.* kidney
río *m.* river
risa *n.* laugh
ritmo *m.* rhythm
rizado *adj.* curly
robar *v. rob;* steal
roca *f.* rock
rojo *n., adj.* red
rollo *m.* roll
romanza *f.* romance
rompecabezas *m.* puzzle
romper *v.* break
ropa *f.* clothes
rosa *n., adj.* pink; *f.* rose
rosado *n., adj.* pink
rubio *adj.* blonde
rueda *f.* wheel
ruido *m.* noise
rural *adj.* rural
ruta *f.* route

S

sábado *m.* Saturday
saber *v. irr.* know (info)
sabor *m.* flavor; taste
saborear *v.* taste
sabroso *adj.* tasty
sacapuntas *f.* pencil
  sharpener
sagrado *adj.* sacred
sal *f.* salt

sala *f.* living room
salado *adj.* salty
salario *m.* salary
salchicha *f.* sausage
salida *f.* exit; departure
salir *v. irr.* exit; leave
saliva *f.* saliva
salmón *m.* salmon
salsa *f.* sauce
saltar *v.* jump
salto *m.* jump
salud *f.* health
salvador *n.* savior
salvaje *adj.* wild
salvar *v.* save
sandalia *f.* sandal
sangre *f.* blood
santo *n.* saint
sapo *m.* toad
satélite *m.* satelite
satisfacción *f.* satisfaction
satisfacer *v. irr.* satisfy
satisfecho *adj.* satisfied
saxafón *m.* saxophone
sección *f.* section
secreto *m.* secret
seguir *v. irr.* continue; follow
segundo *n.* second
seguramente *adv.* surely
seguridad *f.* safety; security
seguro *adj.* certain; sure; safe
sello *m.* stamp
selva *f.* jungle
semáforo *m.* stoplight
semana *f.* week
semanal *adj.* weekly

semejante *m.* similar; like
semestre *m.* semester
semicírculo *m.* semicircle
semilla *f.* seed
senador *n.* senator
señal *f.* sign; signal
sencillo *adj.* plain
Señor *m.* Mr.
Señora *f.* Mrs.
Señorita *f.* Ms.
sensible *adj.* sensitive
sentar(se) *v. irr.* sit
sentido *m.* sense
sentir(se) *v. irr.* feel
separar(se) *v.* separate; split
septiembre *m.* September
séptimo *n., adj.* sixth
ser humano *m.* human
ser *v. irr.* be
serenata *f.* serenade
serie *m.* series
serio *adj.* serious
serpiente *f.* serpent
servicio *m.* service
servilleta *f.* napkin
servir *v. irr.* serve
si *conj.* if
sicólogo *n.* psychologist
siempre *adv.* always
silbar *v.* whistle
silla *f.* chair
símbolo *m.* symbol
sin ebargo *adv.* though
sistema *f.* system
sitio web *m.* website
sobre *prep.* on; onto; over
sobrevivir *v.* survive
sobrina *f.* niece

sobrino *m.* nephew
sofá *f.* sofa
soga *f.* rope
sol *m.* sun
solar *m.* solar
soldado *n.* soldier
solicitar *v.* request
solo *adj.* alone; *adv.* only
solución *f.* solution
solucionar *v.* solve
sombrero *m.* hat
sombrilla *f.* shade; umbrela
soñar *v. irr.* dream
sonido *m.* sound
sonreír(se) *v.* smile
sonrisa *f.* smile
sopa *f.* soup
sorprender *v.* surprise
sorprendido *adj.* surprised
sorpresa *f.* surprise
sospechoso *adj.* suspicious
su *adj.* your
su *pron.* his; her
suave *adj.* smooth
subir *v.* climb
subrayar *v.* underline
suceder *v.* happen
sudar *v.* sweat
sudor *m.* sweat
sudoroso *adj.* sweaty
sueldo *m.* salary
suelo *m.* floor; ground
suerte *f.* luck
suéter *m.* sweater
sufrir *v.* suffer
sugerencia *f.* suggestion
sugerir *v. irr.* suggest
sujeto *m.* subject

superficie *m.* surface
supermercado *m.* supermarket
superstitión *f.* superstition
suponer *v. irr.* suppose
sur *m.* south
surfear *v.* surf
sustituir *v.* substitute; replace
sustraer *v.* subtract
susurra *f.* whisper
susurrar *v.* whisper
suyo *pron.* his; her; yours

T

tachar *v.* delete
talento *m.* talent
talentoso *adj.* talented
talla *f.* size
talón *m.* heel
tamaño *m.* size
también *adv.* also
tambor *m.* drum
tan *adv.* such
taquilla *m.* ticket booth
tarea *f.* homework
tarjeta *f.* card
taxi *m.* taxi
té *m.* tea
teatro *m.* theater
techo interior *m.* cieling
techo *m.* roof
teclado *m.* keyboard
tela *f.* cloth; fabric
telaraña *f.* spiderweb
teléfono *m.* telephone
telescopio *m.* telescope
televisión *f.* television

televisor *m.* television
tema *f.* subject; theme
temblar *v.* quake; shiver
temperatura *f.* temperature
tempestad *f.* storm
templo *m.* temple
tenedor *m.* fork
tener *v. irr.* have
tenis *m.* tennis
teoría *f.* theory
tercero *n., adj.* third
terminar *v.* finish
termómetro *m.*
  thermometer
terreno *m.* terrain
terrible *adj.* terrible
terrífico *adj.* terrific
tesoro *m.* treasure
textear *v.* text (message)
tía *f.* aunt
tiburón *m.* shark
tiempo *m.* time; weather
tienda *f.* store
tierra *f.* dirt; soil; land;
  Earth
tieso *adj.* stiff
tigre *m.* tiger
tijeras *f.* scizzors
tímido *adj.* self-concious;
  shy; timid
tina *f.* tub
tinta *f.* ink
tío *m.* uncle
típico *adj.* tipical
tipo *m.* type
tirar *v.* throw
titular *v.* title
titulo *m.* title

toalla *f.* towel
tobillo *m.* ankle
tocar(se) *v.* touch
tocino *m.* bacon
todavía *adv.* still; yet
todos *adj.* every
tolerancia *f.* tolerance
tolerante *adj.* tolerant
tomar apuntes *v.* take notes
tomar *v.* drink; take
tonelada *f.* ton
torcer(se) *v. irr.*sprain; twist
tornado *m.* tornado
torneo *m.* tournament
toronja *f.* grapefruit
torpe *adj.* clumsy
torre *m.* tower
torta *f.* cake; sándwich
tortilla *f.* tortilla
tortuga *f.* turtle
total *m.* total
totalmente *adv.* totally
trabajador *n.* worker
trabajar *v.* work
trabajo *m.* work
tradición *f.* tradition
tradicional *adj.* traditional
traducción *f.* translation
traducir *v. irr.* translate
tráfico *m.* traffic
tragedia *f.* tragedy
trágico *adj.* trajic
traje *m.* suit
trampa *f.* trick
tranquilidad *f.* traquility
tranquillo *adj.* tranquil
transformar *v.* transform

transparente *adj.* clear;
  transparent
transportar *v.* transport
transporte *m.* transportation
trapo *m.* rag
traumático *adj.* traumatic
tremendo *adj.* tremendous
tren *m.* train
trepar *v.* climb
triángulo *m.* triangle
trineo *m.* sled
triste *adj.* sad
trofeo *m.* trophy
trompeta *f.* trumpet
tropical *adj.* tropical
trópico *m.* tropic
truco *m.* trick
tu *adj.* your
tú mismo *pron.* yourself
tú *pron.* you
tuba *f.* tuba
tubo *m.* tub
túnel *m.* tunnel
turismo *m.* tourism
turista *m.* tourist
tuyo *pron.* yours

U

úlcera *f.* ulcer
último *adj.* last; ultimate
un *indef art.* an; a
ungüento *m.* ointment
único *adj.* only, sole
unidad *f.* unity
unido *adj.* united
unificar *v.* unite
uniforme *m.* uniforme
unir(se) *v.* unite

universidad *f.* university;
  college
uña *f.* fingernail
usar *v.* use
usted *pron.* you (formal)
ustedes *pron.* you (plural)
usual *adj.* usual
útil *adj.* helpful; useful
utilizar *v.* utilize
uva *f.* grape

V

vaca *f.* cow
vacación *f.* vacation
vaciar *v.* empty
vacío *adj.* empty
vacuna *f.* vaccine
vacunación *f.* vaccination
vacunar *v.* vaccinate
vainilla *f.* vanilla
válido *adj.* valid
valiente *adj.* brave
valioso *adj.* valient
valle *m.* valley
valor *m.* valor
vals *m.* waltz
valuar *v.* value
variado *adj.* varied
variedad *f.* variety
varón *m.* man
vaso *m.* glass (cup)
váter *m.* toilet
vecino *n.* neighbor
vegetal *m.* vegetable
vegetariano *n.* vegetarian
vehículo *m.* vehicle
vela *f.* candle
velero *m.* sailboat

velocidad *f.* velocity
vender *v.* sell
venir *v. irr.* come
venta *f.* sale
ventana *f.* window
ver *v. irr.* see
verano *m.* summer
verbo *m.* verb
verdad *f.* truth
verdadero *adj.* true; real
verde *adj., n.* green
verdura *f.* vegetable
vereda *f.* sidewalk
vergüenza *n.*
  embarrasment; shame
verificar *v.* verify
versión *f.* version
vesitir(se) *v. irr.* dress
vestido *m.* dress
veterano *n.* veteran
veterinario *n.* veterinarian
viajar *v.* travel
viaje *m.* trip
vidrio *m.* glass
viejo *adj.* old
viento *m.* wind
viernes *m.* Friday
vinagre *m.* vineger
vino *m.* wine
violín *m.* violin
virus *m.* virus
visión *f.* vision
visita *f.* visit
visitar *v.* visit

viuda *f.* widow
viudo *m.* widower
vivo *adj.* alive
vocabulario *m.* vocabulary
volar *v. irr.* fly
volcán *m.* volcano
voleibol *m.* volleyball
voltear(se) *v.* turn around
volumen *m.* volume
volver *v. irr.* return
votar *v.* vote
voz *f.* voice
vuelo *m.* flight

W

wat *m.* watt

X

xilófono *m.* xylophone

Y

y *conj.* and
ya *adv.* already
yate *m.* yacht
yo *pron.* I

Z

zona *f.* zone
zoológico *m.* zoo

English-Spanish Dictionary

A

able *v.* poder

about *prep.* acerca de; respeto a

above *prep.* sobre; encima de; arriba de

absent *adj.* ausente

accept *v.* aceptar

accident *n.* accidente

accompany *v.* acompañar

ache *n.* dolor; *v.* doler

achieve *v.* lograr; realizar

actor *n.* actor

actress *n.* actriz

adapt *v.* adaptar(se)

add *v.* sumar; añadir

address *n.* dirección

admire *v.* admirar

adopt *v.* adoptar

adult *n.* adulto

adventure *n.* aventura

adventurous *adj.* aventurero

advice *n.* consejo; aviso

affectionate *adj.* cariñoso

afraid *adj.* miedoso; tener miedo

after *prep.* después

afternoon *n.* tarde

again *adv.* otra vez; de nuevo

against *prep.* contra

age *n.* edad

agency *n.* agencia

agent *n.* agente; representante

agree *v.* acordar(se); estar de acuerdo con

agreement *m.* acuerdo

agriculture *n.* agricultura

ahead *adv.* al frente; adelante

air *n.* aire

airplane *n.* avión

airport *n.* aeropuerto

alarm *n.* alarma

alert *adj.* alerta

alien *n.* extraterrestre

alive *adj.* vivo

all *n., adj., pron,* todo

allergy *n.* alergia

allow *v.* permitir

almost *adv.* casi

alone *adj.* solo

along *adv.* junto

alphabet *n.* alfabeto; abecedario

already *adv.* ya

also *adv.* también; ademas

although *conj.* aunque

aluminum *n.* aluminio

always *adv.* siempre

amazing *adj.* maravilloso

ambition *n.* ambición; aspiración

ambitious *adj.* ambicioso

American *adj.* americano

among *prep.* en medio de

ancient *adj.* antiguo

and *conj.* y

angel *n.* ángel

angry *adj.* enojado

animal *n.* animal

ankle *n.* tobillo

annoy *v.* fastidiar
another *adj., pron.* otro
answer *v.* contestar; responder
ant *n.* hormiga
antibiotic *n.* antibiótico
antique *adj.* antiguo
anxious adj. ansioso; inquieto
any *adj., pron.* algún, cualquiera
anybody *pron.* alguien
anyone *pron.* alguien; alguno
anything *pron.* cualquier cosa; alguna cosa
apologize *v.* disculpar(se)
appear *v.* aparecer
apple *n.* manzana
appreciate *v.* apreciar
approve *v.* aprobar
April *n.* abril
aquarium *n.* acuario
architect *n.* arquitecto
argument *n.* argumento
arm *n.* brazo
around *adv.* alrededor
arrive *v.* llegar
art *n.* arte
artist *n.* artista
as *conj., adv.* como
at *prep.* en
ask *v.* preguntar, pedir
asleep *adj.* dormido
aspirin *n.* aspirina
assemble *v.* juntar; reunir
at *prep.,* a; en
athlete *n.* atleta

attend *v.* asistir a
attention *n.* atención
attitude *n.* actitud
August *n.* agosto
aunt *n.* tía
author *n.* autor
avenue *n.* avenida
avocado *n.* aguacate
avoid *v.* evitar
awake *v.* despertar(se)

B

baby *n.* bebé
back *n.* espalda
backpack *n.* mochila
backward *adv.* hacia atrás
bacon *n.* tocino
bad adj. malo
bag *n.* bolsa
bake *v.* cocer en horno
bakery *n.* panadería
balance *v.* balancear
bald *adj.* calvo
ball *n.* pelota; bola
ballet *n.* ballet
banana *n.* plátano
bandaid *n.* curita
bank *n.* banco
barber *n.* peluquero
bargain *v.* regatear
bark *v.* ladrar
barn *n.* granero; establo
baseball *n.* béisbol
basic *adj.* básico
basket *n.* canasta
basketball *n.* baloncesto
bat *n.* murciélago
bathe *v.* bañar(se)

bathing suit *n.* traje de baño
bathroom *n.* baño
bathtub *f.* bañera
battery *n.* pila
bay *n.* bahía
be *v.* estar; ser
beach *n.* playa
beans *n.* frijoles
bear *n.* oso
beard *n.* barba
beautiful *adj.* hermoso; bonito
beauty *n.* belleza
because *conj.* porque
become *v.* hacerse
bed *n.* cama
bedroom *n.* cuarto; dormitorio
bee *n.* abeja
beef *n.* carne de res
before *prep.* antes de
begin *v.* empezar, comenzar
beginning *n.* principio; comienzo
behavior *n.* comportamiento
behind *prep.* detrás de
believable *adj.* creíble
believe *v.* creer
bell *n.* campana
below *prep.* debajo de
belt *n.* cinturón
beneath *prep.* debajo de
besides *prep.* además de
best *adj.* mejor
better *adj.* mejor
between *prep.* entre

beverage *n.* bebida
bicycle *n.* bicicleta
big *adj.* grande
bill *n.* cuenta
billboard *n.* cartelera
biology *n.* biologia
bird *n.* pájaro
birthday *n.* cumpleaños
black *n., adj.* negro
blanket *n.* cobija
block *n.* cuadra
blond *adj.* rubio
blood *n.* sangre
blouse *n.* blusa
blue jeans *n.* blue jeans
blue *n., adj.* azul
boat *n.* barco; bote
body *n.* cuerpo
bone *n.* hueso
book *n.* libro
book store *n.* librería
bookmark *n.* marcador
bookshelf *n.* estantería
boot *n.* bota
bored *adj.* aburrido
boring *adj.* aburrido
born *adj.* nacido
borrow *v.* prestar
boss *n.* jefe
botany *n.* botánica
both *adj., pron.* los dos; ambos
bother *v.* molestar
bottle *n.* botella
boy *n.* niño; muchacho; chico
boyfriend *n.* novio
brain *n.* cerebro

branch *n.* rama
brave *adj.* valiente
bread *n.* pan
break *v.* quebrar; romper
breakfast *n.* desayuno
bridge *n.* puente
bright *adj.* brillante; claro
bring *v.* traer
broken *adj.* roto; quebrado
bronze *n.* bronce
broom *n.* escoba
brother *n.* hermano
brown *n., adj.* café
browser *n.* navegador
brush *n.* cepillo
bug *n.* insecto; bicho
build *v.* construir
building *n.* edificio
bull *n.* toro
burglar *n.* ladrón
bus *n.* autobús;
   autobús escolar (school)
business *n.* negocio
busy *adj.* ocupado
but *conj.* pero
butcher shop *n.* carnicería
butter *n.* mantequilla
butterfly *n.* mariposa
button *n.* botón
buy *v.* comprar
by *prep.* por

C

cabin *n.* cabaña
cable *n.* cable
cactus *n.* cacto
cage *n.* jaula
cake *n.* pastel; torta

calculate *v.* calcular
calculator *n.* calculadora
calendar *n.* calendario
call *v.* llamar
calm *adj.* tranquilo;
   v. tranquilizar
cane *n.* bastón
camera *n.* cámara
camp *v.* acampar
canal *n.* canal
cancel *v.* cancelar
cancer *n.* cáncer
candle *n.* vela
candy *n.* dulce
candy store *n.* dulcería
canoe *n.* canoa
canyon *n.* cañón
capital *n.* capital
captain *n.* capitán
car *n.* coche; carro; auto
caramel *n.* caramelo
card *n.* tarjeta
cardboard *n.* cartón
career *n.* carrera; profesión
careful *adj.* cuidadoso
carnival *n.* carnaval
carousel *n.* carrusel
carpenter *n.* carpintero
carpet *n.* alfombra; tapete
carrot *n.* zanahoria
carry *v.* llevar; cargar
cartoon *n.* caricatura
cash *n.* dinero; efectivo
cashier *n.* cajero
castle *n.* castillo
cat *n.* gato
catch *v.* atrapar; coger
caterpillar *n.* oruga

cathedral *n.* catedral
cause *n.* razón; causa
caution *v.* advertir
cave *n.* cueva; gruta
cavern *n.* caverna
celebrate *v.* celebrar
celebration *n.* celebración
celery *n.* apio
cell phone *n.* teléfono
  celular
cemetary *n.* cementerio
cent *n.* centavo
center *n.* centro
centigrade *adj.* centígrado
centimeter *n.* centimetro
central *adj.* central
ceramic *n.* cerámica
cereal *n.* cereal
ceremony *n.* ceremonia
certain *adj.* seguro; cierto
certainly *adv.* ciertamente
certainty *n.* certeza
certificate *n.* certificado
chair *n.* silla
champion *n.* campión
championship *n.*
  campionato
chance *n.* oportunidad
change *v.* cambiar
channel *n.* canal
chapter *n.* capítulo
charity *n.* caridad
chase *v.* perseguir
chat *v.* charlar
cheap *adj.* barato
cheat *v.* engañar
check *n.* cheque; cuenta
cheek *n.* mejilla

cheer *v.* animar
cheese *n.* queso
chef *n.* cocinero,
  jefe de la cocina
cherry *n.* cereza
chess *n.* ajedrez
chew *v.* masticar
chicken *n.* pollo
child *n.* niño
children *n.* hijos
chili *n.* chile
chimney *n.* chimenea
chin *n.* barbilla
chocolate *n.* chocolate
choir *n.* coro
choose *v.* escojer
chop *v.* cortar
chores *n.* quehaceres
christmas *n.* navidad
church *n.* iglesia
cieling *n.* techo interior
cinnamon *n.* canela
circle *n.* círculo
circus *n.* circo
citizen *n.* ciudadano
citizenship *n.* ciudadanía
city block *n.* cuadra
city *n.* ciudad
clam *n.* almeja
clap *v.* aplaudir
class *n.* clase
clay *n.* barro
clean *v.* limpiar
clear *adj.* transparente;
  claro
climate *n.* clima
climb *v.* subir; trepar
clinic *n.* clínica

clock *n.* reloj
close[1] *v.* cerrar(se)
close[2] *adj.* cerca; cercano
closed *adj.* cerrado
closet *n.* armario
cloth *n.* tela
clothes *n.* ropa
cloud *n.* nube
cloudy *adj.* nublado
clown *n.* payaso
clumsy *adj.* torpe
coast *n.* costa
coat *n.* abrigo
cocoa *n.* cacao
coconut *n.* coco
coffee *n.* café
coin *n.* moneda
cold *n., adj.* frío
collect *v.* coleccionar
collection *n.* colección
college *n.* colegio; universidad
color *v.* colorear; *n.* color
comb *v.* peinar; *n.* peine
combination *n.* combinación
combine *v.* combinar
come *v.* venir; llegar
comedy *n.* comedia
commercial *n.* comercial
common *adj.* común
communicate *v.* comunicar(se)
community *n.* comunidad
compact *adj.* compacto
companion *n.* compañero
company *n.* compañía
compare *v.* comparar

compartment *n.* compartimiento
compass *n.* compás
compete *v.* competir
competition *n.* competencia
complain *v.* quejar(se)
complaint *n.* queja
complement *n.* complemento
complete *adj.* completo
complicate *v.* complicar
comprehend *v.* comprender
computer *n.* computadora
computer science *n.* computación
concert *n.* concierto
condition *n.* condición
confess *v.* confesar
confidence *n.* confianza
confirm *v.* confirmar
confuse *v.* confundir
congratulation *n.* felicitación
connect *v.* conectar
conserve *v.* conservar
consider *v.* considerar
contamination *n.* contaminación
continue *v.* seguir; continuar
contribute *v.* contribuir
control *v.* controlar; dirigir
conversation *n.* conversación
cook *v.* cocinar; *n.* cocinero
cookie *n.* galleta
cool *adj.* fresco
copper *n.* cobre

copy *v.* copiar
corn *n.* maíz;
elote (on the cob)
corner *n.* esquina
correct *v.* corregir
cost *v.* costar; *n.* precio
cotton *n.* algodón
couch *n.* sofá
count *v.* contar
country *n.* país;
campo (countryside)
couple *n.* pareja; par
courageous *adj.* valiente
cousin *n.* primo
cow *n.* vaca
crab *n.* cangrejo
cracker *n.* galleta
crayon *n.* crayón
crazy *adj.* loco
cream *n.* crema
create *v.* producir; crear
creative *adj.* creativo
creature *n.* criatura
credible *adj.* creíble
cricket *n.* grillo
crime *n.* crimen
crocodile *n.* cocodrilo
cross *n.* cruz; *v.* cruzar
crossword puzzle *n.*
crucigrama
crush *v.* aplastar
cry *v.* llorar
crystal *n.* cristal
culture *n.* cultura
cup *n.* taza; vaso
cure *n.* cura
curiosity *n.* curiosidad
curious *adj.* curioso

curly *adj.* rizado
curtain *n.* cortina
curve *n.* curva
custard *n.* flan
custom *n.* costumbre
customer *n.* cliente
cut *v.* cortar; *adj.* cortado;
n. cortadura
cute *adj.* lindo; mono
cycling *n.* ciclismo

D

dad *n.* papá
daily *n.* diaro
dance *v.* bailar
danger *n.* peligro
dangerous *adj.* peligroso
dark *adj.* obscuro;
n. obscuridad
dark hair *adj.* moreno
date *n.* fecha
daughter *n.* hija
day *n.* día
dead *adj.* muerto
death *n.* muerte
December *n.* diciembre
decide *v.* decidir
decorate *v.* decorar
decoration *n.* decoración
deep *adj.* profundo; hondo
degree *n.* grado
dehydrate *v.* deshidratar
delet *v.* tachar
delicious *adj.* delicioso;
rico; sabroso
deliver *v.* entregar
democracy *n.* democracia
demonstrate *v.* mostrar(se)

dense *adj.* denso
dentist *n.* dentista
department store *n.* almacén
departure *n.* salida
deport *v.* deportar
depression *n.* depresión
depth *n.* profundidad
descend *v.* bajar; descender
describe *v.* describir
desert *n.* desierto
deserve *v.* merecer
desk *n.* escritorio; pupitre (student)
despite *prep.* a pesar de
dessert *n.* postre
dial *v.* marcar (número telefónico)
dialogue *n.* diálogo
diamond *n.* diamante
diary *n.* diario
dictionary *n.* diccionario
die *v.* morir
difference *n.* diferencia
different *adj.* diferente; distinto
difficult *adj.* difícil
digestion *n.* digestión
dining room *n.* comedor
dinner *n.* cena
direction *n.* dirección
disappear *v.* desaparecer
discount *n.* descuento
discover *v.* descubrir
discussion *n.* discusión
disease *n.* enfermedad
dish *n.* plato

disinfectant *n.* desinfectante
disk *n.* disco
disobey *v.* desobedecer
distance *n.* distancia
distract *v.* distraer
divide *v.* dividir(se)
do *v.* hacer
doctor *n.* médico; doctor
document *n.* documento
dog *n.* perro
doll *n.* muñeco
dollar *n.* dólar
dolphin *n.* delfín
donkey *n.* burro
door *n.* puerta
doubt *n.* duda; *v.* dudar
down *prep., adv.* abajo
download *v.* descargar
downtown *n.* centro
dozen *n.* docena
drama *n.* drama
draw *v.* dibujar
dream *v.* soñar
dress *v.* vestir(se); *n.* vestido
drink *v.* beber; tomar; *n.* bebida
drive *v.* manejar, conducir
driver *n.* chofer
drug *n.* droga
drum *n.* batería; tambor
duck *n.* pato
during *prep.* durante
DVD *n.* DVD

E

each *adj.* cada

eagle *n.* águila
ear *n.* oreja
early *adv.* temprano
earn *v.* ganar: merecer
earring *n.* arete
earth *n.* tierra
east *n.* este
easy *adj.* fácil
eat breakfast *v.* desayunar
eat dinner *v.* cenar
eat lunch *v.* almorzar
eat *v.* comer
echo *n.* eco
ecological *adj.* ecológico
economic *adj.* económico
economy *n.* economia
edge *n.* orilla
edible *adj.* comestible
edit *v.* editar
educate *v.* educar
education *n.* educación
effect *v.* efectuar;
   n. resultado
effective *adj.* efectivo
efficient *adj.* eficiente
effort *n.* esfuerzo
egg *n.* huevo
either *adj.* cualquiera
elbow *n.* codo
elect *v.* elegir
electricity *n.* electricidad
elegant *adj.* elegante
elephant *n.* elefante
email *n.* correo electrónico
embarrased *adj.*
   avergonzado
emigrate *v.* emigrar
emotion *n.* emoción

employ *v.* emplear
employee *n.* empleado
empty *v.* vaciar; *adj.* vacío;
   desocupado
end *n.* final; fin
energy *n.* energía
engineer *n.* engeniero
English *n.* inglés
enjoy *v.* disfrutar
enormous *adj.* enorme
enough *adv.* bastante
enthusiasm *n.* entusiasmo
entire *adj.* entero; completo
entrance *n.* entrada
environment *n.* medio
   ambiente
episode *n.* episodio
equal *v.* igualar; *n.* igual
equipment *n.* equipo
erase *v.* borrar
eraser *n.* goma de borrar
error *n.* error
eruption *v.* erupción
especially *adv.*
   especialmente
estimate *v.* estimar
ethical *adj.* ético
evacuation *n.* evacuación
evaluate *v.* evaluar
every *adj.* todos; cada
everyday *adj.* todos los días
evidence *n.* evidencia
exact *adj.* exacto
exaggeration *n.*
   exageración
examin *v.* examinar
example *n.* ejemplo
excellent *adj.* excelente

excited *adj.* emocionado
exercise *n.* ejercicio;
  v. hacer ejercicio
exist *v.* existir
exit *v.* salir; *n.* salida
expedition *n.* expedición
experience *n.* experiencia
experiment *n.* experimento
explain *v.* explicar
explanation *n.* explicación
exploration *n.* exploración
explore *v.* explorar
explorer *n.* explorador
explosion *n.* explosión
extinct *adj.* extincto
extra *adj.* extra
extreme *adj.* extremo
eye *n.* ojo
eyebrow *n.* ceja
eyelash *n.* pestaña

F

fabric *n.* tela
fabulous *v.* fabuloso
face *n.* cara
fact *n.* hecho
fail *v.* fallar
fair *adj.* justo
faith *n.* fé
fall (asleep) *v.* dormir(se)
fall (in love) *v.*
  enamorar(se)
fall (season) *n.* otoño
fall *v.* caer(se)
false *adj.* falso
fame *n.* fama
familiar *adj.* familiar
family *n.* familia

famous *adj.* famoso
fan *n.* aficionado
far *adv.* lejos
farm *n.* granja
fascinated *adj.* fascinar (le)
fast *adv.* rápidamente;
  adj. rápido
fat *adj.* gordo
father *n.* padre
fault *n.* culpa
favor *n.* favor
favorite *adj.* favorito
fear – *n.* miedo; temor;
  v. temer
feather *n.* pluma
February *n.* febrero
federal *n.* federal
feel *v.* sentir(se)
female *n.* hembra
feminine *adj.* feminino
festival *n.* fiesta
festive *adj.* festivo
fever *n.* fiebre
few *adj.* poco
fiction *n.* ficción
fifth *n., adj.* quinto
fight – *v.* pelear; luchar,
  n. pelea; lucha
file *m.* archivo
fill *v.* llenar
film *n.* película
final *adj.* final
finally *adv.* finalmente;
  por último; por fin
find out *v.* averiguar
find *v.* encontrar
finger *n.* dedo
fingernail *n.* uña

finish *v.* terminar; acabar
fire *n.* fuego
first *n., adj.* primero; primer
fish *v.* pescar; *m.* pez
 (alive); pescado (cooked)
fish market *n.* pescadería
fix *v.* arreglar
flag *n.* bandera
flame *n.* llama
flat *adj.* plano
flavor *n.* sabor
flexible *adj.* flexible
flight *n.* vuelo
floor *n.* suelo; piso
flour *n.* harina
flower *n.* flor
flute *n.* flauta
fly *v.* volar; *n.* mosca
fog *n.* niebla; neblina
fold *v.* doblar
folder *n.* carpeta
follow *v.* perseguir; seguir
font *n.* tipo de letra
food *n.* comida
foot *n.* pie
football *n.* fútbol americano
for *prep.* para; por
forbid *v.* prohibir
force *v.* forzar; *n.* fuerza
foreign *adj.* extranjero
foreigner *n.* extranjero
forest *n.* bosque
forget *v.* olvidar(se)
forgive *v.* perdonar
fork *n.* tenedor
forward *adv.* adelante
fountain *n.* fuente
fourth *n., adj.* cuarto

fox *n.* zorro
fragile *adj.* frágil
free *v.* libertar (set free);
 adj. libre (unbound);
 gratis (cost)
freeway *n.* autopista;
 carretera
french fries *n.* papas fritas
French *n.* francés
frequent *adj.* frecuente
fresh *adj.* fresco
Friday *n.* viernes
friend *n.* amigo
friendly *adj.* amistoso
frog *n.* rana
from *prep.* desde; de
front *n.* frente
fruit *n.* fruita
frustrated *adj.* frustrado
full *adj.* completo; lleno
fun *adj.* divertido
function *v.* funcionar
funny *adj.* cómico; chistoso

G

galaxy *n.* galaxia
gallon *n.* galón
game *n.* juego; partido
 (sport)
garaje *n.* garaje
garbage *n.* basura
garden *n.* jardín
garlic *n.* ajo
gas *n.* gasolina
generous *adj.* generoso
gentleman *n.* caballero
geography *n.* geografía
get *v.* obtener; conseguir

ghost *n.* fantasma
giant *adj.* gigantesco
gift *n.* regalo
girl *n.* niña; chica; muchacha
girlfriend *n.* novia
give *v.* dar
glad *adj.* alegre
glass *n.* vaso (drinking); vidrio
glasses *n.* gafas; lentes
glove *n.* guante
glue *v.* pegar; *n.* pegamento
go *v.* ir
goat *n.* cabra
god *n.* dios
godfather *n.* padrino
godmother *n.* madrina
godparents *n.* padrinos
gold *n.* oro
golf *n.* golf
good *adj.* bien; bueno
goodbye *n. interj.* adiós
goose *n.* ganso
gossip *n.* chisme
gossiper *adj.* chismoso
governor *n.* gobernador
grade *n.* grado (school level); nota (school report)
grand *adj.* magnífico
grandchild *n.* nieto
grandfather *n.* abuelo
grandmother *n.* abuela
grandparents *n.* abuelos
grape *n.* uva
grapefruit *n.* toronja
grass *n.* hierba; pasto; césped

great *adj.* fenomenal
green *adj., n.* verde
grey *adj., n.* gris
grey haired *adj.* canoso
groceries *n.* comestibles
grocery store *f.* tienda de comestibles
ground *f.* suelo
grow *v.* crecer
guacamole *n.* guacamole
guitar *n.* guitara
gym *n.* gimnasio
gymnastics *n.* gimnasia

H

habit *n.* costumbre; hábito
habitat *n.* hábitat
hail *n.* granizo;
hair *n.* pelo; cabello
hallway *n.* corredor; pasillo
ham *n.* jamón
hamburger *n.* hamburguesa
hand *n.* mano
handsome *adj.* guapo
hang *v.* colgar
happen *v.* pasar; suceder
happy *adj.* feliz; contento; alegre
harbor *n.* puerto
hard *adj.* difícil; duro
harm *v.* dañar
harvest *v.* cosechar
hat *n.* sombrero; gorro; gorra
hate *v.* chocar (le); odiar
have *v.* tener
hay *n.* paja
he *pron.* él

head *n.* cabeza
health *n.* salud
hear *v.* oír
heart *n.* corazón
heat *v.* calentar; *n.* calor
heaven *n.* cielo
heavy *adj.* pesado
heel *n.* talón
height *n.* altura; estatura
helicopter *n.* helicóptero
hello *int.* hola
help *n.* ayuda; *v.* ayudar
helpful *adj.* útil
her *pron.* suyo; de ella; su
here *adv.* aquí
hero *n.* héroe
heroic *adj.* heroico
hide *v.* esconder(se)
high *adj.* alto
high school *n.* colegio;
  preparatoria
hike *n.* caminata
hill *n.* cerro
himself *pron.* él mismo
hip *n.* cadera
his *pron.* suyo; de él; su
history *n.* historia
hit *n.* golpe; *v.* golpear
hockey *n.* hockey
hold *v.* detener
holiday *n.* día festivo
home *n.* casa; hogar
homework *n.* tarea
honest *adj.* honesto;
  honrado
honey *n.* miel
hope *v.* desear, esperar;
  n. esperanza

horror *n.* horror
horse *n.* caballo
hospital *n.* hospital
hot adj. caliente, *n.* calor
  (weather)
hotel *n.* hotel
hour *n.* hora
house *n.* casa
how *adv.* cómo
how many? *inter.*
  ¿Cuántos?
how much? *inter.*
  ¿Cuánto?
how? *inter.* ¿Cómo?
hug *n.* abrazo; *v.* abrazar
huge adj. enorme
human *n.* ser humano
humid *adj.* húmedo
hunger *n.* hambre
hunt *v.* cazar
husband *n.* esposo
hysterical *adj.* histérico

I

I *pron.* yo
ice cream *n.* helado
ice *n.* hielo
idea *n.* idea
identification *n.*
  identificación
if *conj.* si
illness *n.* enfermedad
illusion *n.* ilusión
imaginative *adj.*
  imaginativo
imagine *v.* imaginar
imitate *v.* imitar
immature *adj.* inmaduro

immense *adj.* inmenso
immigrate *v.* inmigrar
impatient *adj.* impaciente
impolite *adj.* descortés
importance *n.* importancia
important *adj.* importante
impossible *n.* imposible
improve *v.* mejorar
in *prep.* en
inch *n.* pulgada
incomplete *adj.* incompleto
incorrect *adj.* incorrecto
increase *v.* aumentar
independence *n.*
  independencia
indigestion *n.* indigestión
indingenous *n.* indígena
individual *n.* individuo
infect *v.* infectar
infection *n.* infección
inflate *v.* inflar
inform *v.* informar
information *n.* información
ink *n.* tinta
innocent *adj.* inocente
insect *n.* insecto
inspection *n.* inspección
inspiration *n.* inspiración
instruction *n.* instrucción
insulin *n.* insulina
intelligent *adj.* inteligente
interest *n.* interés
interesting *adj.* interesante
internet *n.* internet
into *prep.* en; a
introduce *v.* introducir
investigate *v.* investigar
invisible *adj.* invisible

invitation *f.* invitación
invite *v.* invitar
island *n.* isla
itinerary *n.* itinerario

J

jacket *n.* chaqueta
jaguar *n.* jaguar
jail *v.* encarcelar, *n.* cárcel
January *n.* enero
jar *n.* jarra
jaw *n.* mandíbula
jazz *n.* jazz
jealous *adj.* celoso
jelly *n.* jalea
jeopardize *v.* arriesgar;
  poner en peligro
jewelry *n.* joyas
jewelry store *n.* joyería
job *n.* trabajo
join *v.* unir(se); juntar(se)
journal *n.* diario
journalist *n.* periodista
judge *n.* juez; *v.* juzgar
juice *n.* jugo
July *n.* julio
jump *n.* salto; *v.* saltar
June *n.* junio
jungle *n.* selva
justify *v.* justificar

K

keep *v.* guardar; detener;
key *n.* llave
keyboard *n.* teclado
kidney *n.* riñón
kilogram *n.* kilogramo
kilometer *n.* kilómetro
kind *adj.* cariñoso

king *n.* rey
kiss *n.* beso; *v.* besar
kitchen *n.* cocina
kitten *n.* gatito
knee *n.* rodilla
knife *n.* cuchillo
know[1] *v.* saber (facts/info)
know[2] *v.* conocer
   (person/place)

L

ladder *n.* escalera
lady *n.* dama
lagoon *n.* laguna
lake *n.* lago
lamb *n.* cordero; borrego
lamp *n.* lámpara
land *n.* tierra
landscape *n.* paisaje
language *n.* lenguaje
large *adj.* grande
last *adv.* finalmente;
   adj. final; último
late *adv.* tarde
laugh *n.* risa, *v.* reír(se)
law *n.* ley
lawyer *n.* abogado
lazy *adj.* flojo; perezoso
leader *n.* líder
leaf *n.* hoja
learn *v.* aprender
least *adv.* menos
leave *v.* salir; irse
left *adj.* izquierdo
leg *n.* pierna
legal *adj.* legal
legend *n.* leyenda
lemon *n.* limón

lemonade *n.* limonada
less *adj.* menos
lesson *n.* lección
let *v.* dejar; permitir
letter *n.* carta; letra
   (alphabet)
lettuce *n.* lechuga
liberty *n.* libertad
library *n.* biblioteca
lie *n.* mentira; *v.* mentir;
   acostar(se) (lie down)
life *n.* vida
lift *v.* levantar(se)
light *n.* luz
like *n.* semejante; igual;
   v. gustar
like *v.* gustar (le)
lime *n.* lima
limit *v.* limitar
line *n.* línea
lion *n.* león
lip *n.* labio
liquid *n.* liquido
list *n.* lista
listen *v.* escuchar
literature *n.* literatura
little *n., adv.* poco;
   adj. pequeño
live *v.* vivir
living room *n.* sala
lobster *n.* langosta
long *adj.* largo
look for *v.* buscar
look; *v.* mirar: *n.* mirada
lose *v. irr.* perder
lost *adj.* perdido
lotion *n.* loción

loud *adj.* alto (voice);
fuerte (sound)
love *v.* amar; querer;
encantar (le) *n.* amor
lovely *adj.* lindo
luck *n.* suerte
luggage *n.* equipaje
lunch *n.* almuerzo
v. irr. almorzar

M

machine *n.* máquina
mad *adj.* enojado
magazine *n.* revista
magic *n.* mágica
magnetic *adj.* magnético
mail *n.* correo
maintain *v.* mantener
majority *n.* mayoría
make *v.* hacer
malnutrition *n.*
desnutrición
man *n.* hombre; varón
manage *v.* manejar;
administrar
mandatory *adj.* obligatorio
mango *n.* mango
manner *n.* manera
many *adj.* muchos
map *n.* mapa
March[1] *n.* marzo
march[2] *v.* marchar
marina *n.* marina
mark *n.* marca
marker *n.* marcador
market *n.* mercado
marriage *n.* matrimonio
marry *v.* casar(se)

marvellous *adj.*
maravilloso
mascot *n.* mascota
masculine *adj.* masculino
material *n.* material
math *n.* matemáticas
mature *v.* madurar;
adj. maduro
May *n.* mayo
me *pron.* me
meal *n.* comida
mean *adj.* antipático
measure *v.* medir
measurement *n.* medida
meat *n.* carne
mechanic *n.* mecánico
medal *n.* medalla
medicine *n.* medicina
meet *v.* reunir(se);
encontrar(se) con
melody *n.* melodía
member *n.* miembro
memorize *v.* aprender de
memoria
memory *n.* memoria
mention *v.* mencionar
menu *n.* menú
message *n.* mensaje
metal *n.* metal
microwave *n.* microonda
middle *n., adj.* medio
migrate *v.* migrar
milk *n.* leche
milkshake *n.* batido
minor *n.* menor
minus *prep.* menos
miracle *n.* milagro
mirror *n.* espejo

mission *n.* misión
mistake *v.* equivocar(se)
mister *n.* señor
mistreat *v.* maltratar
mix *n.* mezcla;
    v. mezclar(se)
model *v.* modelar;
    n. modelo
modern *adj.* moderno
mom *n.* mamá
moment *n.* momento
Monday *n.* lunes
money *n.* dinero
monkey *n.* mono; chango
monster *n.* monstruo
month *n.* mes
moon *n.* luna
more *adv. adj.* más
morning *n.* mañana
mosquito *n.* mosquito
mother *n.* madre
motorcycle *n.* motocicleta
mountain *n.* montaña;
    monte
mouse *n.* ratón
mouth *n.* boca
move *v.* mudar; mover
movie *n.* película
movie theatre *n.* cine
Mr. *n.* Señor
Mrs. *n.* Señora
Ms. *n.* Señorita
much *adv.* muy; *adv., adj.*
    mucho
multiplication *n.*
    multiplicación
muscle *n.* músculo
museum *n.* museo

music *n.* música
musician *n.* músico
must *v.* deber
mustache *n.* bigote
my *adj.* mi
myself *pron.* yo mismo
mystery *n.* misterio

N

name *n.* nombre
napkin *n.* servilleta
nation *n.* nación
natural *adj.* natural
nature *n.* naturaleza
nausea *n.* náusea
nautical *adj.* náutico
navigate *v.* navegar
near *prep.* cerca de
    adv. cerca
necessary *adj.* necesario
neck *n.* cuello
necklace *n.* collar
need *v.* necesitar
negative *adj.* negativo;
    n. negativo
neighbor *n.* vecino
neither *pron.* ninguno;
    conj. tampoco; ni
nephew *n.* sobrino
nervous *adj.* nervioso
never *adv.* jamás; nunca
new *adj.* nuevo
news *n.* noticias
next *adj.* luego; próximo;
    a continuación
nice *adj.* amable; simpático
niece *n.* sobrina
night *n.* noche

ninth *n., adj.* novena
no *n., adv.* no
nobody *n., pron.* nadie
noise *n.* ruido
none *pron.* nada
noon *n.* mediodía
nor *conj.* ni
normal *adj.* normal
normally *adv.* normalmente
north *n.* norte
nose *n.* nariz
not adv. no
note *v.* notar; *n.* nota; *pl.* apuntes
notebook *n.* cuaderno
notify *v.* notificar
November *n.* noviembre
now *adv.* ahora
number *n.* número
nurse *n.* enfermero
nut *n.* nuez
nutrition n. nutrición

#

obey *v.* obedecer
occasion *n.* ocasión
occupation *n.* ocupación
occur *v.* ocurrir
ocean *n.* océano
October *n.* octubre
odd *adj.* raro
odor *n.* olor
of *prep.* de
offer *n.* ofrecimiento; *v.* ofrecer
office *n.* oficina
officer *n.* oficial
oil *n.* aceite; petróleo

ointment *n.* pomada
old *adj.* viejo; anciano
older *adj.* mayor
on *prep.* sobre; en
once *n., adv.* una vez
onion *n.* cebolla
online *prep.* en línea
only *adj.* solo; *adv.* sólo
onto *prep.* sobre; en
open *v.* abrir; *adj.* abierto
operation *n.* operación
opinion *n.* opinión
opportunity *n.* oportunidad
opposite *adj.* opuesto
option *n.* opción
or *conj.* o
orange *adj.* anaranjado; *n.* naranja
orchestra *n.* orquestra
order *n.* orden
ordinary *adj.* ordinario
organization *n.* organización
organize *v.* organizar
original *adj.* original
ornament *n.* ornamentos
other *pron., adj.* otro
ounce *n.* onza
our *adj.* nuestro
ourselves *pron.* nostros mismos
out *prep.* fuera de; *adv.* fuera
outside *adv.* afuera; fuera
oval *n.* ovál
oven *n.* horno
over *prep.* sobre; encima de

owl *n.* búho; lechuza; tecolote
oxygen *n.* oxígeno
oyster *n.* ostra

P

pack *v.* empacar
package *n.* paquete
page *n.* página
pain *v.* dolor
paint *v.* pintar; *n.* pintura
painting *n.* pintura
pair *n.* par; pareja
pale *adj.* pálido
palm tree *n.* palma; palmera
pamphlet *n.* folleto
panic *n.* pánico
pants *n.* pantalones
papaya *n.* papaya
paper *n.* papel
parade *n.* desfile
paradise *n.* paraíso
paragraph *n.* párrafo
parents *n.* padres
park *n.* parque; *v.* estacionar
parking *n.* estacionamiento
parrot *n.* loro
participate *v.* participar
party *n.* fiesta
pass *v. irr.* aprobar (an exam); pasar
passenger *n.* pasajero
patio *n.* patio
pay *v.* pagar
peanut butter *n.* crema de maní; crema de cacahuate

peanut *n.* cacahuate
pear *n.* pera
pen *n.* pluma; bolígrafo
pencil *n.* lápiz
pencil sharpener *n.* sacapuntas
penguin *n.* pingüino
people *n.* gente
percent *n.* por ciento
permit *v.* permitir; permiso
pet *n.* mascota
pharmacy *n.* farmacia
photograph *n.* fotografía
phrase *n.* frase
piano *n.* piano
pie *n.* pastel
pig *n.* cerdo; puerco; cochino
pilot *n.* piloto
pineapple *n.* piña
pink *n., adj.* rosado; rosa
place *n.* lugar
plain *adj.* sencillo
plan *v.* planear; *n.* plan
plane *n.* avión
planet *n.* planeta
plant *n.* planta; *v.* plantar
plastic *n., adj.* plástico
plate *n.* plato
play *v.* tocar (instrument); jugar (game);
player *n.* jugador
pleasure *n.* placer
plenty *n.* abundancia
plum *n.* ciruela
plural *n., adj.* plural
plus *n.* más
pocket *n.* bolsillo

poem *n.* poema
poet *n.* poeta
police *n.* policía
pollution *n.* polución
pond *n.* estanque; charca
pool *n.* piscina; alberca
poor *adj.* pobre
popular *adj.* popular
porcelain *n.* porcelana
position *n.* posición
positive *adj.* positivo
possible *adj.* possible
post office *n.* correo
poster *n.* póster; cartel
potato chips *n.* papitas
potato *n.* papa; patata
pound *n.* libra
poverty *n.* pobreza
power off *v.* apagar;
   adj. apagado
power on *v.* encender;
   adj. encendido
practice *v.* practicar
precaution *n.* precaución
prefer *v.* preferir
preference *n.* preferencia
preoccupied *adj.*
   preocupado
prepare *v.* preparar(se)
prescribe *v.* prescribir;
   recetar
prescription *n.* receta
present *v.* presentar;
   n. regalo; *adj.* presente
president *n.* presidente
pretend *v.* pretender
pretty *adj.* bonito; mono
prevent *v.* prevenir; impedir

price *n.* precio; costo
pride *n.* orgullo
primary *adj.* primario
primitive *adj.* primitivo
principal *adj.* principal;
   n. director
print *v.* imprimir
printer *n.* impresora
private *adj.* privado
prize *n.* premio
probable *adj.* probable
problema *n.* problema
procedure *n.* procedimiento
process *n.* proceso
product *n.* producto
profession *n.* profesión
professor *n.* profesor
program *n.* programa
progress *n.* progreso
prohibit *v.* prohibir
project *n.* proyecto
promise *v.* prometer;
   n. promesa
pronounce *v.* pronunciar
proof *n.* prueba
property *n.* propiedad
protect *v.* proteger
proud *adj.* orgulloso
prove *v.* probar
provide *v.* proveer
psychiatrist *n.* psiquiatra
psychologist *n.* sicólogo
public *n., adj.* público
publish *v.* publicar
puddle *n.* charco
pull *v.* jalar
pulmonary *adj.* pulmonar
pulse *n.* pulso

pumpkin *n.* calabaza
purchase *v.* comprar
pure *adj.* puro
purple *n., adj.* morado
purpose *n.* propósito
purse *n.* bolsa
pursue *v.* perseguir
push *v.* empujar
put *v.* poner(se)
puzzle *n.* rompecabezas
pyramid *n.* pirámide

Q

quake *v.* temblar
qualification *n.* cafilicación
quality *n.* calidad
quantity *n.* cantidad
quarter *n.* cuarto
queen *n.* reina
question *n.* pregunta
quick *adj.* rápido
quiet *adj.* quieto; callado
quit *v.* dejar; irse;
    descontinuar
quiz *n.* prueba

R

rabbit *n.* conejo
race *n.* carrera
racism *n.* racismo
racist *n.* racista
racoon *n.* mapache
radio *n.* radio
radish *n.* rábano
raffle *n.* rifa
rag *n.* trapo
railing *n.* baranda
railroad *n.* ferrocarril
railway *n.* ferrocarril

rain forest *n.* selva tropical
rain *v.* llover; *n.* lluvia
rainbow *n.* arco iris
raincoat *n.* impermeable
rainy *adj.* lluvioso
raise *v.* criar (as a child);
    levantar (lift)
raisin *n.* pasa
ranch *n.* hacienda; rancho
rare *adj.* raro
rasberry *n.* frambuesa
rash *n.* erupción
rat *n.* rata
raven *n.* cuervo
reach *v.* alcanzar
reaction *n.* reacción
read *v.* leer
reading *n.* lectura
ready *adj.* listo
real *adj.* real
realize *v.* realizar;
    darse cuenta de
reality *n.* realidad
really *adv.* realmente
reason *v.* razonar; *n.* razón
reasonable *adj.* razonable
receipt *n.* recibo
receive *v.* recibir
recent *adj.* reciente
recess *n.* recreo; descanso
recipe *n.* receta
rectangle *n.* rectángulo
red *n., adj.* rojo
red-headed *adj.* pelirrojo
reference *n.* referencia
reflect *v.* reflejar
refrigerator *n.* refrigerador
refugee *n.* refugiado

refund *n.* reembolso;
  v. reembolsar
region *n.* región
regret *v.* arrepentir
regular *adj.* regular
relative *n.* pariente
relax *v.* relajar(se)
relieve *v.* aliviar
remember *v.* recordar;
  acordarse de
remind *v.* recordar
remove *v.* quitar(se)
rent *v.* alquilar; *n.* renta
repair *v.* reparar
repeat *v.* repetir(se)
replace *v.* sustituir
reply *v.* repuesta
reptile *n.* reptil
request *v.* solicitar
reservation *n.* reservación
reserve *v.* reservar
resist *v.* resistir
resource *n.* recurso
respect *v.* respetar;
  n. respeto
response *n.* repuesta
respond *v.* responder
responsible *adj.*
  responsable
rest *v.* descansar
restaurant *n.* restaurante
result *n.* resultado
return *v.* volver; regresar
reunion *n.* reunión
review *v.* repasar
reward *n.* premio
rhythm *n.* ritmo
rib *n.* costilla

rice *n.* arroz
rich *adj.* rico
ride *v.* montar
right *adj.* derecho
rip *v.* arrancar
ripe *adj.* maduro
risk *n.* riesgo
river *n.* río
road *n.* camino
rob *v.* robar
rock *n.* roca, piedra
rocket *n.* cohete
roll *n.* rollo
romance *n.* romanza
roof *n.* techo
room *n.* cuarto; habitación
rooster *n.* gallo
root *n.* raíz
rope *n.* cuerda, soga
rose *n.* rosa
round *adj.* redondo
route *n.* ruta
rug *n.* alfombra
rule *n.* regla
ruler *n.* regla
run *v.* correr
rural *adj.* rural

S

sacred *adj.* sagrado
sad *adj.* triste
safe *adj.* seguro
safety *n.* seguridad
sailboat *n.* velero
sailor *n.* marinero
saint *n., adj.* santo
salad *n.* ensalada
salary *n.* salario; sueldo

sale *n.* venta
saliva *n.* saliva
salmon *n.* salmón
salt *n.* sal
salty *adj.* salado
same *adj.* mismo; igual; idéntico
sand *n.* arena
sandal *n.* sandalia
sandwich *n.* bocadillo; emparedado
satellite *n.* satélite
satisfaction *n.* satisfacción
satisfied *adj.* satisfecho
satisfy *v.* satisfacer
Saturday *n.* sábado
sauce *n.* salsa
sausage *n.* salchicha; chorizo
save *v.* ahorrar; salvar: guardar
savior *n.* salvador
saxophone *n.* saxofón
say *v.* decir
saying *n.* dicho
scab *n.* costra
scandal *n.* escándalo
scar *n.* cicatriz
scare *v.* asustar; espantar
scared *adj.* asustado
scarf *n.* bufanda
scenery *n.* paisaje
scent *n.* olor; aroma
schedule *n.* horario
scholarship *n.* beca
school *n.* escuela
science *n.* ciencias
scientist *n.* científico

scizzors *n.* tijeras
scold *v.* regañar
score *n.* cuenta; resultado
scorpion *n.* alacrán; escorpión
scratch *v.* rayar; rasguñar; rascar
scream *v.* gritar; *n.* grito
screen *n.* pantalla (device)
scuba dive *v.* bucear
sculpt *v.* esculpir
sculptor *n.* escultor
sculpture *n.* escultura
sea *n.* mar
seagull *n.* gaviota
seal *n.* foca
search engine *n.* buscador
search *v.* buscar
seasickness *n.* mareo
season *n.* estación
seat *n.* asiento
seaweed *n.* alga marina
second *n., adj.* segundo
secondary *adj.* secundario
secret *n., adj.* secreto
section *n.* sección
see *v.* ver
seed *n.* semilla
self-concious *adj.* tímido
self-confidence *n.* confianza en sí mismo
self-control *n.* dominio de sí mismo
selfish *adj.* egoísta
sell *v.* vender
semester *n.* semestre
semicircle *n.* semicírculo
semicolon *n.* punto y coma

senator *n.* senador
send *v.* enviar; mandar
sense *n.* sentido
sensitive *adj.* sensible; delicado
sentence *n.* oración
separate *v.* separar
September *n.* septiembre
serenade *n.* serenata
series *n.* serie
serious *adj.* serio
serpent *n.* serpiente
serve *v.* servir
service *n.* servicio
seventh *n., adj.* séptimo
several *adj.* varios
severe *adj.* severo; grave
sew *v.* coser
shade *n.* sombra
shadow *n.* sombra
shame *n.* vergüenza
shampoo *n.* champú
shape *v.* formar; *n.* forma
share *v.* compartir
shark *n.* tiburón
sharp *adj.* agudo
shave *v.* afeitar(se)
shawl *n.* chal
she *pron.* ella
sheep *n.* oveja
shelf *n.* estante
shell *n.* concha
shellfish *n.* marisco
shin *n.* espinilla
shine *v.* brillar
shiny *adj.* brillante
ship *n.* barco
shirt *n.* camisa

shiver *v.* temblar
shoe *n.* zapato
shoe store *n.* zapatería
shop *m.* taller; *n.* tienda
shopping mall *n.* centro comercial
short *adj.* breve (time); corto (length); bajo (height)
shorts *n.* pantalones cortos
should *v.* deber
shoulder *n.* hombro
shout *v.* gritar; *n.* grito
show *v.* mostrar(se); demonstrar
shower *v.* duchar(se); *n.* ducha
shrimp *n.* camarón
shut *v.* cerrar(se)
shy *adj.* tímido
sick *adj.* enfermo
sickness *n.* enfermedad
side *n.* lado
sidewalk *n.* vereda
sign *n.* signo; señal
signal *n.* señal
signature *n.* firma
silence *n.* silencio
silk *n.* seda
silver *n.* plata
similar *adj.* similar; parecido
simple *adj.* sencillo; simple
sing *v.* cantar
singer *n.* cantante
sink *n.* fregadero; lavamanos
sister *n.* hermana

sister-in-law *n.* cuñada
sit *v.* sentar(se)
site *n.* sitio
situation *n.* situación
sixth *n., adj.* sexto
size *n.* talla; tamaño
skate *v.* patinar
skateboard *n.* monopatín
skeleton *n.* esqueleto;
  calaca
ski *v.* esquiar
skiing *n.* esquí
skin *n.* piel
skinny *adj.* delgado; flaco
skirt *n.* falda
skull *n.* calavera
sky *n.* cielo
skyscraper *n.* rascacielos
sled *n.* trineo
sleep *v. irr.* dormir(se)
slipper *n.* zapatilla
slow *adj.* despacio; lento
small *adj.* pequeño;
  chiquito
smart *adj.* listo
smell *v.* oler
smile *v.* sonreír(se);
  n. sonrisa
smoke *v.* fumar; *n.* humo
smooth *adj.* suave
snack *v.* merendar
snail *n.* caracol
snake *n.* culebra; serpiente
sneeze *n.* estornudo;
  v. estornudar
snow *v.* nevar; *n.* nieve
snowboard *v.* surfear sobre
  nieve

so *conj.* por lo tanto;
  adv. así; tan
soap *n.* jabón
soccer *n.* fútbol
social science *n.* ciencias
  sociales
sock *n.* calcetín
soda *n.* refresco
sofa *n.* sofá
software *n.* programa
soil *n.* tierra
solar *n.* solar
soldier *n.* soldado
solution *n.* solución
solve *v.* resolver; solucionar
some *pron., adj.* algunos
somebody *pron.* alguien
someday *adv.* algún día
someone *pron.* alguien
something *n.* algo
sometimes *adv.* a veces
son *n.* hijo
song *n.* canción
soon *adv.* pronto
soul *n.* alma
sound *n.* sonido
soup *n.* sopa
sour *adj.* agrio
south *n.* sur
space *n.* espacio
spaghetti *n.* espagueti
Spanish *n.* español
speak *v.* hablar
special *adj.* especial
specialist *n.* especialista
specialize *v.*
  especializar(se)
specialty *n.* especialidad

species *n.* especie
specify *v.* especificar
spectacular *adj.*
  espectacular
spell *v.* deletrear
spelling *n.* ortografía
spend *v.* gastar; pasar (time)
spice *n.* especia
spicy *adj.* picante
spider *n.* araña
spinach *n.* espinaca
spirit *n.* espíritu
split *v.* dividir; separar(se)
spoil *v.* echar(se) a perder
sponge *n.* esponja
spoon *n.* cuchara
sport *n.* deporte
spot *n.* mancha; lugar
spouse *n.* esposa; esposo
sprain *v.* torcer(se)
springtime *n.* primavera
spy *v.* espiar
square *adj., n.* cuadrado
stadium *n.* estadio
stain *n.* mancha
stairs *n.* escaleras
stairway *n.* escalera
stamp *n.* sello; estampilla
stand *v.* estar de pie
staple *n.* grapa
stapler *n.* grapadora
star *n.* estrella
start *v.* empezar; comenzar
state *n.* estado
station *n.* estación
statue *n.* estatua
stay *v.* quedar(se)
steak *n.* bistec

steal *v.* robar
stick *n.* palo
sticky *adj.* pegajoso
stiff *adj.* rígido; tieso
stomach *n.* estómago
stone *n.* piedra
stop *v.* parar; suspender
stoplight *n.* semáforo
store *n.* tienda; almacén
storm *n.* tempestad
story *n.* historia; cuento
stove *n.* estufa
straight *adj.* derecho;
  directo; recto
strange *adj.* extraño; raro
strategy *n.* estrategia
straw *n.* paja;
  popote (drink)
strawberry *n.* fresa
stream *n.* arroyo
street *n.* calle
strength *n.* fuerza
stretch *v.* estirar(se)
strict *adj.* estricto
string *n.* hilo
stripe *n.* raya
striped *adj.* rayado
strong adj. fuerte
student *n.* estudiante
study *v.* estudiar; *n.* estudio
style *n.* modo; estilo
subject *n.* sujeto; tema;
  materia (class subject)
subtract *v.* sustraer
subway *n.* metro
succeed *v.* tener éxito
success *n.* éxito
such *adv.* tan; *pron., adj.* tal

suffer *v.* sufrir
sugar *n.* azúcar
suggest *v.* sugerir
suggestion *n.* sugerencia
suit *n.* traje
summary *n.* resumen
summer *n.* verano
summit *n.* cumbre
sun *n.* sol
Sunday *n.* domingo
sunglasses *n.* lentes de sol; gafas de sol
sunlight *n.* luz de sol
sunrise *n.* salida del sol
sunset *n.* puesta del sol
supermarket *n.* supermercado
superstition *n.* superstición
suppose *v.* suponer
sure *adj.* seguro; cierto
surely *adv.* seguramente
surf *v.* surfear
surface *n.* superficie
surgeon *n.* cirujano
surgury *n.* cirugía
surname *n.* apellido
surprise *v.* sorprender; *n.* sorpresa
surprised *adj.* sorprendido
survive *v.* sobrevivir
suspicious *adj.* sospechoso
sweat *n.* sudor; *v.* sudar
sweater *n.* suéter
sweaty *adj.* sudoroso
sweep *v.* barrer
sweet *adj.* dulce
swim *v.* nadar
swimming *n.* natación

switch *v.* cambiar
sword *n.* espada
symbol *n.* símbolo
system *n.* sistema

T

table *n.* mesa
tablespoon *n.* cuchara
tag *n.* etiqueta
tail *n.* cola
take notes *v.* apuntar; tomar apuntes
take *v.* coger; tomar; sacar
talent *n.* talento
talented *adj.* talentoso
talk *v.* hablar; platicar
tall *adj.* alto
tape *n.* cinta
taste *n.* sabor; *v.* probar; saborear
tasty *adj.* sabroso
taxi *n.* taxi
tea *n.* té
teach *v.* enseñar; educar
teacher *n.* maestro; profesor
team *n.* equipo
tear *n.* lágrima
telephone *n.* teléfono
telescope *n.* telescopio
television *n.* televisión; televisor
temperature *n.* temperatura; fiebre
temple *n.* templo
tennis *n.* tenis
terrain *n.* terreno
terrible *adj.* terrible
terrific *adj.* terrífico

test *v.* examinar; probar
n. examen
text (messaging) *v.* textear
text message *n.* mensaje de
texto
than *conj.* de; que
thankful *adj.* agradecido
thanks *n.* gracias
that *adj.* aquella; aquél;
esa; ese
the *def. art.* la; el; las; los
theatre *n.* teatro
them *pron.* ellas; ellos
theme *n.* tema
then *adv.* luego; entonces
theory *n.* teoría
there *adv.* ahí; allí; allá
thermometer *n.*
termómetro
these *pron.* éstas; éstos;
adj. estos; estas
they *pron.* ellas, ellos
thick *adj.* grueso
thigh *n.* muslo
thin *adj.* delgado
thing *n.* cosa
think *v.* pensar
third *n., adj.* tercero
thirst *n.* sed
this *adj.* esta; este;
pron. esto; ésta; este
though *adv.* sin embargo;
conj. aunque
thoughtful *adj.* pensativo;
atento; considerado
threaten *v.* amenazar
throat *n.* garganta

through *prep.* por; a través
de
throw *v.* tirar; echar; lanzar
thumb *n.* pulgar
Thursday *n.* jueves
ticket booth *n.* taquilla
ticket *n.* boleto
tickle v. cosquillear
tidy up *v.* ordenar
tie *v.* amarrar; *n.* corbata
tiger *n.* tigre
till *prep.* hasta
time *n.* hora; tiempo
timid *adj.* tímido
tip *n.* propina (service);
punta
tire *v.* cansar(se)
tired *adj.* cansado
tissue *n.* pañuelo
title *v.* titular; *n.* título
to *adv., prep.* hacia;
prep. hasta; a
toad *n.* sapo
today *n., adv.* hoy
toe *n.* dedo del pie
together *adv.* junto
toilet *n.* váter; tocador
tolerance *n.* tolerancia
tolerant *adj.* tolerante
tomato *n.* jitomate
tomorrow *adv., n.* mañana
ton *n.* tonelada
tongue *n.* lengua
tonight *n., adv.* esta noche
too *adv.* además; también;
demasiado
tool *n.* herramienta
tooth *n.* diente

toothbrush *n.* cepillo de dientes
toothpaste *n.* pasta de dientes
tornado *n.* tornado
tortilla *n.* tortilla
total *n.* total
totally *adv.* totalmente
touch *v.* tocar(se)
tough *adj.* difícil; duro
toughen *v.* endurecer(se)
tourism *n.* turismo
tourist *n.* turista
tournament *n.* torneo
toward *prep.* hacia
towel *n.* toalla
tower *n.* torre
town *n.* pueblo
track & field *n.* atletismo
tradition *n.* tradición
traditional *adj.* tradicional
traffic *n.* tráfico
tragedy *n.* tragedia
tragic *adj.* trágico
train *n.* tren
tranquil *adj.* tranquilo
tranquility *n.* tranquilidad
transform *v.* transformar
translate *v.* traducir
translation *n.* traducción
transport *n.* transporte; *v.* transportar
transportation *n.* transporte
trash *n.* basura
traumatic *adj.* traumático
travel *v.* viajar
treasure *n.* tesoro

tree *n.* árbol
tremendous *adj.* tremendo
triangle *n.* triángulo
trick *n.* truco; engaño; trampa
trip *n.* viaje
trophy *n.* trofeo
tropic *n.* trópico
tropical *adj.* tropical
truck *n.* camión
true *adj.* verdadero; legítimo
trumpet *n.* trompeta
truth *n.* verdad
try on *v.* probarse
try *v.* probar; intentar
t-shirt *n.* camiseta
tub *n.* bañera; tina
tuba *n.* tuba
tube *n.* tubo
Tuesday *n.* martes
tuna *n.* atún
tunnel *n.* túnel
turkey *n.* pavo
turn around *v.* voltear(se)
turn off *v.* apagar
turtle *n.* tortuga
TV set *n.* televisor
twice *adv.* dos veces
twin *adj.*, *n.* gemelo
twist *v.* torcer(se)
type *n.* tipo
typical *adj.* típico

U

ugly *adj.* feo
ulcer *n.* úlcera
ultimate *adj.* último

umbrella *n.* paraguas;
  sombrilla
umpire *n.* árbitro
unable *adj.* incapaz
unacceptable *adj.*
  inaceptable
unavoidable *adj.* inevitable
unbelievable *adj.* increíble
uncle *n.* tío
uncomfortable *adj.*
  incómodo
uncommon *adj.* raro;
  infrecuente
uncooked *adj.* crudo
underline *v.* subrayar
underneath *adv.* debajo;
  prep. bajo
understand *v.* comprender;
  entender
underwear *n.* ropa interior;
  calzones
uniform *n.* uniforme
unite *v.* unificar; unir(se)
united *adj.* unido
unity *n.* unidad
university *n.* universidad
until *prep.* hasta
unusual *adj.* raro
up *prep.* hacia arriba;
  adv. arriba
upstairs *adv.* arriba
us *pron.* nosotras; nosotros
use *n.* uso; *v.* utilizer; usar
useless *adj.* inutíl;
useful *adj.* útil
usual *adj.* usual
utilize *v.* utilizar

V

vacation *n.* vacación
vaccinate *v.* vacunar
vaccination *n.* vacunación
vaccine *n.* vacuna
valid *adj.* válido
valley *n.* valle
valor *n.* valor
valuable *adj.* valioso
value *v.* valuar; *n.* valor
vanilla *n.* vanilla
variety *n.* variedad
various *adj.* variado;
  numerosos
vegetable *n.* legumbre;
  vegetal; verdura
vegetarian *n.* vegetariano
vehicle *n.* vehículo
velocity *n.* velocidad
verb *n.* verbo
verify *v.* verificar
version *n.* versión
very *adv.* muy; mucho
vest *n.* chaleco
veteran *adj., n.* veterano
veterinarian *n.* veterinario
vinegar *n.* vinagre
violin *n.* violín
virus *n.* virus
vision *n.* visión
visit *n.* visita; *v.* visitar
vocabulary *n.* vocabulario
voice *n.* voz
voicemail *n.* mensaje
  de voz
volcano *n.* volcán
volleyball *n.* voleibol

volume *n.* volumen
vote *v.* votar

W

waist *n.* cintura
wait *v.* esperar
waiter *n.* camarero; mesero
wake *v.* despertar(se)
walk *n.* caminata;
　v. caminar; andar
wall *n.* pared
wallet *n.* cartera
walrus *n.* morsa
waltz *n.* vals
want *v.* querer
warehouse *n.* almacén
warm *v.* calentar(se);
　adj. caluroso
warmhearted *adj.* cariñoso
warn *v.* advertir; avisar
warning *n.* advertencia;
　aviso
warrior *n.* guerrero
was *pret. of* be; ser, estar
wash *v.* lavar(se)
wasp *n.* avispa
waste *v.* desperdiciar;
　n. pérdida
watch *n.* reloj; *v.* mirar
water *n.* agua
waterfall *n.* cascada
wave *n.* ola
wax *n.* cera
we *pron.* nosotras; nosotros
weak *adj.* débil
weakness *n.* debilidad
wealth *n.* riqueza
wear *v.* llevar; traer puesto

weather *n.* tiempo; clima
web *n.* telaraña; tejido
website *n.* sitio web
wedding *n.* boda
wednesday *n.* miércoles
week *n.* semana
weekend *n.* fin de semana
weekly *adj.* semanal
weigh *v.* pesar
weight *n.* pesa; peso
welcome *adj.* bienvenido
well *adv.* pues; *adj.* bien
west *n.* oeste
wet *v.* mojar(se)
whale *n.* ballena
what *pron.* lo que; cuál
what? *interr.* ¿qué?
wheel *n.* rueda
wheelchair *n.* silla de
　ruedas
when *adv., conj.* cuando
when? *interr.* ¿cuándo?
where *adv.* donde; adonde;
　por donde
where? *interr.* ¿dónde?;
　¿adónde?
wherever *adv.* dondequiera
　(que)
whether *conj.* si
which *pron.* lo que; cuál
whichever *pron.* cualquiera
while *conj.* mientras (que)
whiskers *n.* barbas; bigotes
whisper *n.* susurra;
　cuchicheo; *v.* susurrar;
　cuchichear
whistle *v.* silbar
white *n., adj.* blanco

who *pron.* el (la, los, las)
 que; quién(es); que
who? *inter.* ¿quién?;
¿quiénes? (plural)
whoever *pron.* quienquiera
 (que)
whole *adj.* entero
whom *pron.* a quien
whomever *pron.*
 quienquiera (que)
whose *pron.* de quien(es);
 de quién(es)
why *adv.* por que
why? *inter.* ¿por qué?
wide *adj.* ancho
widow *n.* viuda
widower *n.* viudo
wife *n.* esposa
wild *adj.* salvaje
win *v.* ganar
wind *n.* viento
window *n.* ventana
wine *n.* vino
wing *n.* ala
winner *n.* ganador
winter *n.* invierno
wire *n.* alambre
wise *adj.* sabio
wish *n.* deseo; *v.* desear
witch *n.* bruja
with *prep.* con
withstand *v.* aguantar
wolf *n.* lobo
woman *n.* mujer
wonder *v.* asombrar(se);
 maravillar(se)
wood *n.* madera
wool *n.* lana

word *n.* palabra
work *v.* trabajar; *m.* trabajo
worker *n.* trabajador
world *n.* mundo
worm *n.* gusano; lombriz
worn *adj.* usado; gastado
worried *adj.* preocupado/a
worry *v.* preocupar(se)
worse *adj.* peor
wrist *n.* muñeca
write *v.* escribir
wrong *adj.* equivocado

X

x-ray *v.* radiografiar;
 n. radiografía

Y

yact *n.* yate
yard *n.* yarda
yawn *v.* bostezar; *n.* bosteza
year *n.* año
yell *n.* grito; *v.* gritar
yellow *n., adj.* amarillo
yes *adv.* sí
yesterday *n., adv.* ayer
yet *adv.* todavía; aún
you *pron.* tú; usted; ustedes
young *adj.* joven
younger *adj.* menor
your *adj.* su/s; tu/s;
 de usted(es)
yours *pron.* tuyo/a; suyo/a;
 de usted o ustedes
yourself *pron.* usted mismo;
 tú mismo

Z

zebra *n.* cebra

zero *n.* cero
zone *n.* zona
zoo *n.* zoológico
zucchini *n.* calabacín

NOTES / APUNTES:

NOTES / APUNTES:

Made in the USA
San Bernardino, CA
24 September 2018